ACCLAIM

for

UNDER THE GREAT ELM

"Actor/singer /songwriter/poet Flanders documents an adventurous life well lived in his sweeping and deeply honest memoir.

Flanders spins beautiful prose as he recounts his life's journey...Readers will live vicariously through the author's varied, adventurous life, which has an abundance of adventure and braveness packed into it. Any reader who believes in second chances and living life to the fullest will devour Flanders's tale...His Renaissance Man life will inspire readers to realize that it's never too late to chase a dream."

BOOKLIFE

"Appropriately subtitled, 'A Life of Luck & Wonder,' Rich Flanders' memoir, *UNDER THE GREAT ELM*, chronicles his days of world travel, spiritual searching, and romantic serendipity with an infectious sense of amazement and curiosity.

We have a fascination for people who live life on their own terms and Flanders definitely fits that bill; hitchhiking all over America doing odd jobs to survive, wandering through Paris on an LSD trip, and selling blood to finance trips through Greece, Turkey, and Israel are just a few of his exploits.

Flanders' curiosity, wonder, and joy shine through the narrative...a lifelong session of 'Mystery School.'"

4 STARS
(out of 5)
INDIE READER

For all its bucolic roots, *Under the Great Elm* is like an explosion as the narrator moves his experience from rural to urban roots, encounters military and spiritual challenges that both stymie him and open his eyes to the world, and brings readers along on a ride that moves from past lives to present and future expectations.

The sea changes and journey move author and readers through spiritual, psychological, and physical changes that shake the foundations of belief and perception alike as the saga moves from America to India and Europe.

The sense of wonder, enchantment, and growth that accompany these journeys provides armchair readers with a 'you are there' feel of emotional transformations that are engrossing and, often, unexpected.

The result is a literary piece that belongs in a range of collections, from those that feature autobiographical explorations to others that focus on spiritual or psychological growth opportunities, and the search for a place to truly call home."

MIDWEST BOOK REVIEW
D. Donovan, Senior Reviewer

**"Evincing a carpe diem attitude,
Under the Great Elm is a globe-trotting memoir."**

"Rich Flanders's memoir Under the Great Elm is about a life of adventure and love—as well as a healthy dose of luck.

Opening with his childhood and weaving toward the present, Flanders recounts his life stories with immersive lyricism. The book engages the senses in recalling cozy Parisian bookstores, kibbutz feasts, and a household garden. Visceral descriptions of less comfortable settings are also a draw, as with a traumatic childhood field trip and the persistent pain of grief.

Throughout the book, Flanders delights in everyday pleasures and embraces whatever circumstances he finds himself in...Flanders' prose is propulsive and surprising, featuring unexpected turns of phrase, like 'I'd sold my blood to pay for the boat passage to Haifa.' Powerful simplicity is preferenced in the book's descriptions of moments of vulnerability—including around Flanders's loss of his first wife: 'We were one. Now I was half.' Later, a rekindled love is captured in terms of the tender ease of their unspoken understanding.

Evincing a carpe diem attitude, *Under the Great Elm* is a globe-trotting memoir."

***FOREWORD CLARION REVIEWS*,** Danielle Ballantyne

For Lisa
– This tale of Love
Quest and Light
– Best of Luck Always
Rich Flanders
4/11/22

UNDER THE GREAT ELM

A LIFE OF LUCK & WONDER

RICH FLANDERS

Copyright © 2022 by Rich Flanders

ISBN: 978-1-73796-840-5 Paperback
ISBN: 978-1-73796-841-2 Hard cover
ISBN: 978-1-73796-842-9 eBook

Yondering Star Press

To contact the author:
www.richflandersmusic.com

For Anne

What is love? 'tis not hereafter;

Present mirth hath present laughter;

What's to come is still unsure:

In delay there lies no plenty;

Then come kiss me, sweet-and-twenty!

Youth's a stuff will not endure.

William Shakespeare, *Twelfth Night*

My mother, keeping an eye on her son exploring the banks of the Fox River, Illinois, early 1940s.

CONTENTS

Want the change. Be inspired by the flame
where everything shines as it disappears.
The artist, when sketching, loves nothing so much
as the curve of the body as it turns away.

What locks itself in sameness has congealed.
Is it safer to be gray and numb?
What turns hard becomes rigid
and is easily shattered.

Pour yourself like a fountain.
Flow into the knowledge that what you are seeking
finishes often at the start, and, with ending, begins.

Every happiness is the child of a separation
it did not think it could survive. And Daphne, becoming a laurel,
dares you to become the wind.

Rainer Maria Rilke, *Sonnets to Orpheus*

PREFACE

Some stories long to be told, especially when the narrator needs to hear it.

This one, a tale of love, adventure, and near miraculous encounters, seemed like a series of unconnected moments, scattered fragments of familiar songs. I wrote this story to make sense of the wildly diverse events of my life.

Perhaps because of the sudden nature of some of these experiences, my sense of continuity, of time and place, was nebulous. Looking at the aging, tattered books on the shelves one day, I said to Anne that the reason I had held onto them for so many years was not only because of their impact on me. Each book was also a lamp lighting up a place and time in my life, reminding me of where I was, and who I was when I read it.

Beyond the evocations prompted by these books, I needed to find some sort of a through-line for my life. So, I began to write, and remember, and as my story unfolded, I marveled at the wondrous moments and uncanny luck that has graced my journey.

This is a story about trusting the heart. It is a love song, but not just of a young man and woman who met and lost each other in the tumult and color of the 1960s. It's a song of crashing rivers, the scent of honeysuckle, the call of a wolf.

It is a tale of riding loosely on the winds of change, embracing the unknown, and leaping into the current.

In the spirit of wonder,

Rich

CHAPTER 1:
UNDER THE GREAT ELM

Bands of Sauk and Fox may have passed under its soaring boughs, maybe even Black Hawk himself. The great tree surely had been there for a couple of hundred years by the time my dad moved our family to the little brick house in the meadow near the railroad tracks, just after the war. It was mine to lie under on the balmy bursting days of spring, the cool hazy autumn, and the languorous summer. Gazing up through the leaves to the blue Illinois sky, as I lay beside its rugged trunk, I watched the limbs stretch high above and listened to the wind in the swaying branches. The great elm was my companion through the prairie years.

"Watch Johnny Lemon die!"

No matter what she was doing, my mother would hurry outside whenever she heard Johnny was about to die. It was a beautiful sight. "Shot" by cap gun, he would freeze atop the picnic table, spin, pitch forward, and fall loosely to the grass in lifeless glory. From Westerns, gangster movies, and war pictures, Johnny had perfected the slow, dramatic death falls of outlaws, mobsters, and Nazis. Agile and wiry, he could have grown up to be a Hollywood stuntman. The death falls of Johnny Lemon were spectacular.

In 1947, my playmates in the bucolic little Illinois town of Western Springs were Johnny, who, in addition to being a dying gunman, was a crackerjack pitcher; solemn John Ritzman, whose dad had been killed in action two years before in Germany; Spencer, my inseparable best friend who lived up the street; and Bob Ludeke, our German refugee schoolmate whose hands shook constantly. During his family's escape flight from Germany near the end of the war, antiaircraft and machine-gun fire had riddled the airplane, narrowly missing him and his mother and father. They managed to land safely in France, and then emigrated to Western Springs, but Bob Ludeke would tremble for years.

Our classmates, especially John Ritzman, were not always kind to Bob in the bitter days after the war. Unfortunately for Bob, our second-grade teacher was Mrs. Ritzman, John's widowed mother. She could be extra harsh in her rebukes for any real or imagined transgressions of this young German stranger to our land. So it was that I took a liking to him, an early manifestation of an urge to protect the underdog. It was probably thanks to my mother that I developed an eye for those who are left out or get left behind—the less fortunate ones. She had an uncanny knack for noticing them when no one else would. She'd see them hidden in the frames of the movies we saw together, or she'd spot them in a random crowd as we drove along an avenue. "Oh, that poor guy."

On a sunny late summer morning, Bob and I were careening with abandon down the slope of Franklin Avenue on our bikes, headed toward my red brick house at the end of the road. When Mrs. Morgan waved at me from her living room window, I waved back, having been taught to always be polite. I was to pay dearly for that courtesy. Smiling at Mrs. Morgan, I missed seeing the parked car ahead, and my speeding bike crashed into it. I flew headfirst over the handlebars straight into the shattering headlight. The splinters ripped across my forehead. Screaming with pain and blinded by the blood pouring into my eyes, I ran for my life toward my house at the end of the road.

My mother, still recovering from the cesarean birth of my baby sister, fainted when she saw me. I may owe my life to our neighbor, Mrs. Herkus, who happened to hear the clamor and see the gory scene outside her window. She grabbed towels and dialed the emergency number. Then she hurried over to me and soaked up blood, while also tending to my mother until the medics arrived. They pulled up in the town's one fire truck, three or four young men recently back from the war. Flashing smiles of reassurance and comforting me with kind words, they calmed my terror. When they carried me, semi-conscious, to the bright new fire truck, I could hardly believe it. All the way to the sanitarium, which served as our town's emergency room, their smiling faces beamed down as they distracted me with the gadgets of their prized new truck. They knew how to please a boy. They knew about wounds and blood.

At the sanitarium the doctor probed my head for glass fragments, and then with thick black thread, he slowly stitched up the long gashes across my forehead. Because of the jaggedness of the wounds, the stitching was irregular and took focus and time. I dimly sensed the silent presence of my mother and dad behind me in the room.

I would be confined to bed for many days, forbidden to touch the bandages over my head. So, naturally, I did. I stole out of bed to take a peek one afternoon and was thrilled to see the thick, bright scars that were forming. I would be marked, different, an outsider! No other kid had scars like this!

Bob Ludeke's dad was a skilled woodworker, and one of our Cub Scout meetings took place in the Ludeke basement. Mr. Ludeke, surrounded by exotic tools, tried in vain to corral our unruly squad and instruct us. Ignoring him, we set about carving our own splintery, lopsided, Picassoesque versions of wooden spoons and bowls.

Bob's parents were kind and gracious to me—grateful, I suppose, that I had befriended their son. Mr. Ludeke would take Bob and me on evening fishing trips to the pond at Harvester Farms, where he worked as a mechanic. Sitting by the pond in the summer twilight with my bamboo pole over the water, watching the surface ripple now and then from a rising bluegill or bass, I drank in the scent of honeysuckle and listened to the symphony of frogs, crickets, and night birds. Catching something didn't matter.

I felt that same stirring of soul when our class took a field trip to a nearby dairy farm. As I walked among the munching, slow moving cows, jumped over the brook, and came upon a quiet pond with darting blue-green dragonflies, mud turtles, and bull frogs sitting alert, I was just a fellow critter. The rich smell of manure and stacked hay in the barnyard were a kind of perfume for me. The red farm buildings, happy running dogs, and rows of tall waving corn spoke deeply and quietly, calling me to stay on, to live in that world.

The great elm out back would be okay with that.

Through the years my mother would sometimes quietly observe, "You ought to be a farmer, Rich." But I'd also shown some musicality at five years old. One Sunday morning my startled parents awoke to the plaintive serenade of "In the Garden" floating down the hall:

And he walks with me and he talks with me, and he tells me I am his own,
and the joy we share as we tarry there, none other has ever known . . .

I was also making progress on my grandfather's old trumpet. He'd made his living playing in orchestras around Chicago and Aurora. In later years, noticing that singing and acting was a good fit for me, my mother ceased reminding me of farming. But the farmer never left.

Years later, my first wife and I would attempt to recreate a bucolic life at an old farmhouse on Van Auken Creek in Pennsylvania, and later in the rolling Hudson Valley of New York. There we tilled the loamy black soil and grew robust vegetables and herbs. Our furred and feathered relations helped us with the harvests, and they were always welcome on their land.

If that class field trip to the dairy farm had been a paean to the wonders of nature on our little patch of Illinois prairie, our next field trip was the direct opposite. I suppose the school thought it would be a good idea to take the kids to the Chicago Stock Yards, hoping to inspire the upcoming generation with the industrial might and progress of fast-moving, post-war America. I count myself fortunate to have had the experience, one I wish the world could have shared.

Even before the bus pulled into the vast, dusty complex of holding corrals, you could hear the bellowing of terrified cattle. Pressed impossibly close together, they fell over each other and pushed violently against the gates, desperate from the scent of death in the air. When the bus stopped and we filed out, a cheerful, seemingly oblivious guide led a group of wide-eyed seven and eight-year-olds through the slaughterhouses. With his nonchalant detachment, our guide could just as easily have been a Nazi leading a tour of the concentration camps. It was a scene of such horrific irony that Kurt Vonnegut might have had difficulty capturing it. With clammy hands and our stomachs in knots, we were walked with care and precision past each station. Even now I see the men in hip boots standing knee-deep in blood, as wide-eyed, screaming cows are lifted in harnesses onto the conveyor belt and carried steadily toward the big man with the sledgehammer. I see him swing and connect, see the man at the next station working deftly with the long knives. Then on to the pigs, and the same deadly sequence. "Oh, and see how they make sausage, kids?"

They were scenes unfit for the vilest horror movie, but this was not a movie. The images blasted our hearts and seared our memories forever. For weeks afterwards, deeply despondent, I couldn't eat the meat served at dinner, no matter how hungry I was. It wasn't a matter of principle or willpower. My whole body simply recoiled.

In the days following, I often lay out back under the great elm. Our tree soared so high I had to strain my eyes to see the top. Its trunk was so thick, three of us could disappear behind it. Through snow or rain, baking sun, howling winds...or screaming pigs, the elm stood everlasting.

I am forever thankful for that field trip, and almost regret that the Stockyards were taken down. If enough people could have seen what we saw that day, it might have created generations of vegans, saved countless cows, steers, pigs, and sheep, and slowed the warming of the planet.

At around four o'clock every afternoon, I would stand in our front yard waiting for the bright orange California Zephyr to roar by. The engineer, in his blue striped cap, would lean out the window and wave. Outside of this fleeting hello to that faraway state, movies were our only window to the West, our only chance to escape the soul-deadening flatness of Illinois and glimpse towering mountains, rolling plains, cactus studded deserts, and horsemen against the sky.

In the summer of 1946, our family drove to the Black Hills of South Dakota for a vacation. In the forests of those rolling, blue-black mountains, I remember the scent of pine and feeling a deep glow of contentment. The memory of the Black Hills lingered as I grew older, and I smiled inside whenever I thought of them. It was a country that set the heart beating, and as an adventuring teenager I would be lured back to those mountains. Through the years, as I learned about the Sioux and Cheyenne, I discovered that the Black Hills were, in fact, sacred ground; they were the legendary birthplace of the tribes. No wonder I had felt something special there as a child. I sometimes also wonder if part of the joy I felt in those Black Hills at five years old was knowing in some mystical way that my future mate was being born in a New York hospital at the very same time.

Five years old, 1946

Every year on my birthday my spirit soared as we drove to nearby Le Grange to see the latest Roy Rogers picture in Technicolor. In addition to being "out West" for a while, we were going to see and hear Roy Rogers and the Sons of the Pioneers! We had to stand in a line that wound all around the block, girls and boys with their folks, all as excited as I was. Like many of the kids of those times, I longed to live on that ranch up on the screen with Roy and the Pioneers. In their music were faraway mountains under sweeping skies, the scent of pinon pine, the feel of rawhide. It was a haunting blend that penetrated my soul and inspired me, decades later, to create my own albums.

The grace and rhythms of the swing band era also flowed through those years. My dad, fresh from playing in the Big Bands of the late thirties and early forties, formed a couple of small bands of his own. The musicians rehearsed in our front living room. Time and again I would run in from playing outside, only to come face to face with rows of music stands and strange men with instruments, crammed together in that little room; my dad up front, violin nearby, leading the rehearsal. One New Year's Eve, when I was supposed to be fast asleep in my bedroom just off the living room, friends from my dad's band days showed up with their instruments. Wide awake into the wee hours, I listened in a glow to the "jamming" of fine musicians and beat time to irresistible rhythms. The music of the "Great American Songbook," along with the music of the West, would pulse in my blood from then on.

Will Flanders (left) with the Guardsmen, backing up Wee Bonnie Baker of the Orrin Tucker Orchestra, circa 1939.

Then Roy Rogers came to town. Well, not exactly to our town, but to the big city of Chicago, not too far away. It was a show celebrating the "King of the Cowboys" that was touring all around the country at that time. Somehow my dad had procured tickets. Roy and his horse, Trigger, did tricks, and Roy sang a couple of songs. At one point in the show, he doffed his hat and announced to the thousands of kids and their folks:

"Now, I'm gonna' take a ride all around the stadium and shake hands with all the little buckaroos."

Pandemonium . . . a mass of kids and their dads strained and tangled with each other to get to the edge of the crowd at the front to shake Roy's hand. Bless my dad. Hoisting me onto his shoulders he somehow pushed his way through that screaming melee and secured a spot right at the railing. I could see Roy and Trigger working their way down the arena, that ever-present, sunny smile on Roy's face as he stopped to shake hands and say a few words with every girl and boy who could reach him. Finally, he was just feet away, and when he came to me, I'll never forget the moment. Looking straight into my eyes he grasped my small hand, smiled, and said in his soft, easy Western voice, "Howdy, pardner!" If there were such a thing as a Western "darshan" (meeting one's guru) this was it. Something happens when someone you hold in the highest esteem takes a moment in time, just for you, and looks directly into your eyes. It was a formative event.

Aside from rare nights out at the movies, we had the radio. After school on a fall day, Spencer and I would run up the road to his house through swirling gold and orange leaves in time to catch *Sergeant Preston of the Yukon*. We hunched up beside the bureau that housed the radio and listened in tense silence, while his mother placed steaming cups of Ovaltine within reach.

On Saturday mornings, sprawled on the rug, I fell into the world of *Let's Pretend*, and gleefully guffawed at the sassy backtalk and delicious retorts that Buster Brown and Froggy the Gremlin made to their elders. On Sunday evenings we smiled at the humor of *Henry Aldrich, Our Miss Brooks*, and the Jack Benny show. After dinner on weeknights, I saw far horizons and heard the thundering hoofbeats and the sonorous bass voice of *The Lone Ranger.*

The meadows were full of critters and rabbits hiding in clumps of purple and yellow iris. Every spring I would go looking for the wild iris, intoxicated by their scent and colors. But on Saturday mornings, no matter how engaged we were in exploring the fields, Spencer and I would bolt to his house in time to see Hopalong Cassidy on a fantastic new device.

Sometime in 1949 television exploded on our street, making its first appearance in Spencer's home. Flash Gordon and Don Winslow movie serials from the 1930s comprised most of the programming on the one operating channel, but the station also featured the films of Hopalong Cassidy. Dressed in unlikely black, Hopalong Cassidy had white hair and a booming laugh, and eyes that spoke the difference between right and wrong. Dangerous, beguiling at the same time, this jovial, deadly Westerner was irresistible. We were his every Saturday morning.

When *King Solomon's Mines* came out in Technicolor in 1950, it was a sensation to the kids in our village, where our only images of the outside world came through movies and magazines. Here, bursting before our eyes in bright color, was Africa, with its wondrous leopards, zebras, ostriches, giraffes, cheetahs, elephants, wildebeests, lions, rhinos, hyenas, antelope, huge spiders and gigantic snakes. We were riveted, our blood pounding.

That same year, as it happened, my dad was faced with a momentous decision. The company he worked for had offered him a transfer. He was going to have to choose between San Francisco or the new office in Johannesburg, South Africa. I could hardly believe it. Moving to Africa! I had just seen its plains and jungles teeming with wild, beautiful animals. The idea that we were actually going to be living there was electrifying.

My dad chose San Francisco.

The late summer breeze was warm, but I felt a chill as I drew my hand along the weathered bark and lay down beside the tree.

I would say goodbye to the great elm, and much more.

But that's another story...

Norman Rockwell America, Rich (left) and pals, 1950.

CHAPTER 2:
THE GOLDEN HILLS

Everything you love will eventually be lost, but in the end,
love will return in another way.

—Franz Kafka

Along the slow, winding Fox River, box turtles sunned on the bank and golden carp flashed in the eddies. Farther out under the dark current, catfish, two and three feet long, cruised over the muddy bottom. The river teemed with life in the years after the war. It was a place of wonder and delight.

My cousins lived in a three-story, wood-framed house alongside the river in the nearby town of Batavia. When my parents dropped me off for my yearly summer visit, I burst out of the car, my suitcase packed with shorts and t-shirts flying behind me.

Wry and witty, my older cousin Butch kept me laughing as we explored in the cattails and willows along the river or trekked up the elm and maple-lined avenue to see Randolph Scott in *Man in the Saddle*. Evenings might find us sitting on the porch catching lightning bugs and sipping "black cows," while the river lapped softly by.

Now, inconceivably, we were leaving Illinois. In the late summer of 1951, the big Hudson backed out of the driveway of our home in Western Springs for the last time. On the grass, my pal Spencer waved in bewilderment. In the bushes, our cat Tippy was nursing her newborn kittens. With my face pressed against the window, I screamed in panic, "Who will feed her? Who's gonna' take care of the kittens?" In the summer breeze, the great elm waved a final time. As we crossed the Fox River and headed for California, these would be my last images of Illinois. They would haunt me all the long drive across the land.

In those days, the hills of San Mateo rippled with tall golden grass, dotted here and there by dark green clumps of juniper and live-oak. Cattle grazed freely across the slopes, interrupted only by the sprawl of a Japanese orchard.

In the years after the move, tramping through those hills would be a healing balm. But in the shock of those first weeks, I found myself on a cold playground below the railroad tracks, aching for Illinois, trying not to cry. There was no time for grief. I was the new kid in odd-looking country clothes, and ranged before me were laughing, hulking boys who longed to test my mettle. Palms sweating, heart racing, I was alone with no escape. As if in a dream, a carelessness rose within me. The sniggering boys closing in had no clue of the mounting danger before them. The one out front lunged. With the wild energy of fear, I struck my attacker, and under a flurry of frantic blows he covered his face and staggered backward.

It ended as quickly as it had begun. Stunned by the desperate ferocity of the new kid, the boys backed off. I had earned their respect, and the right to be left alone.

The sudden uprooting from Western Springs had been an amputation, not a gradual separation. As the early 1950s rolled by, the sunny, country boy turned inward and became alienated. At one point I fell into a mysterious, undiagnosed fever and sleep-like illness.

Desperate scenes would play out in those first years after the move, like the time George Braun, the older kid up the street, along with his burly sidekick, stole my bike. Though troubled by the odds, my mother pushed away her concerns to let me know I had to "stand up for myself." When George rode by on my bike, taunting me, any fear I had was replaced by outrage. I ran outside and the next moment found myself in a flurry of swinging fists with a larger, stronger antagonist. Neighbors began to gather silently on the lawn, staring at the desperate abandon of the smaller boy. The outcome seemed preordained, but George was taken aback by my fury and the occasional blow that slipped past his guard. As the minutes wore on, the silence broken only by ragged breathing, the smack of fists, and my tearful curses, George slowly began to tire, while I somehow refused to go down. Suddenly, unexpectedly, he held up his hand and breathlessly stammered, "I... I've had enough if you have."

It was an astonishing moment, as much of a "victory" as I could ever have imagined. But still in the grip of wild hopelessness, instead of seizing the opportunity to end the fight, I swung again. Disgusted, and with renewed determination, George's fist connected, knocking me down. As I dragged myself up, I spotted his pal smirking on the edge of the crowd. As if taking on one over-sized bully wasn't enough, I charged at his accomplice in a blind rage, screaming swear words whose meaning eluded me, and hit him in the jaw. Unfazed, he launched a heavy, seasoned punch that sent me flying into the grass. With bitter tears streaming down my face, I staggered home through the silent onlookers.

While tending to my wounds, my mother praised me for having done what was right and for "sticking up for myself." It must not have been easy for her to see her boy outmatched in pitched battle with tough older kids. But somehow, she knew this was a moment that had to be seen through.

Roy and Hopalong clapped me on the shoulder, beaming sunny western smiles. Like my folks, they expected me to fight for the right, to always pick myself up when down, and to keep going.

Later that afternoon, George Braun wheeled my bike up to our porch and quietly knocked on the door. A half-smile hitched up the corner of his mouth as he held out his hand, saying he was sorry to have taken my bike, and maybe we could be friends.

In the hot, still days of Illinois summers, I'd sometimes put up a lemonade stand. I was continually dreaming up enterprises. Once, inspired by a passing carnival, I created a slapdash version of my own carnival in the back yard, featuring games, rides, and adventures, and grabbed unsuspecting kids after school and charged them five cents admission.

Now behind the house in San Mateo, I found old boards and pieced together a lopsided shack. There I could escape to read science fiction and Westerns by Will Henry and Louis L'Amour.

One day, as I sat alone in the shack, avoiding the trickle of rain seeping through the roof, I thought, why not turn this into something? Maybe a shop of some sort. How about a "fixit shop"? The name sounded great, even though I knew nothing about "fixing" anything.

I passed the word around, then proceeded to sit at my "desk" in the shop, whittling and waiting for clients. A bemused neighbor finally brought me something to "fix." Startled into having to suddenly be an actual repair guy, I picked up the object with care and consideration, tinkered with it using an old screwdriver and a pair of pliers, and upon a thorough investigation of the implement, backwards and forwards, upside down and all around, I announced firmly, "This can't be fixed."

And so ended my days in the "fixit" business.

When I was nearing twelve, too old not to have learned to swim, my parents enrolled me in group lessons at the YMCA on Saturday mornings. Terrified of deep water, I was the kid who froze in the shallow end when the rest of the class ventured into the deeper water. I was an embarrassment, not progressing with the other kids.

Lesson after lesson, week after week, I still wouldn't venture into the deep water.

Then one Saturday morning, I walked out of the dressing room to confront rows of families, with several young girls sitting in the stands. It was "family day," and parents and siblings were there to watch us display our skills in the pool. Adolescence suddenly reared its head and vanity eclipsed fear. I wasn't about to be a wimp in front of pretty girls. When the instructor blew his whistle from the other side of the pool, signaling the class to paddle over to him, he expected I would hang back as usual. With a quick glance at the girls in the gallery, I took a deep breath and dove in headfirst, splashing wildly for the other side. Ignoring the gaping instructor, I nonchalantly joined the rest of the class as if I did this every day.

Fear of deep water was gone. I had learned to swim. But most important, I hadn't disgraced myself!

At Borel Junior High, Connie Sheehan was the chief hood. Tall and curly haired, he had probably flunked out at least twice and was now several inches taller and a couple years ahead of the rest of us. During the lunchtime baseball game, several of the kids on the other team openly cheated and, unfortunately, my sense of justice erupted.

The bell rang and as we walked to our classrooms, I burned with outrage and impulsively yelled at the tall kid walking up ahead with the team of cheaters: "You *~(#@ so and so!" I had no idea who it was I had yelled at or what the words meant; only that they were the worst curse words I could come up with.

The big fellow halted and slowly turned around, bemused, and pointed to himself: "Speakin' to me?"

Students fell back, clearing a path between us, and suddenly I was clammy all over, realizing I was face to face with Connie Sheehan, the most feared kid in school.

Smiling, he quietly asked again, "What'd you call me?"

There was no escape now, and in a barely audible monotone, I repeated the epithet. His fist shot out, and my head rolled back. My vision swimming, I managed to swing back. The brief moments in which we tangled seemed like an eternity. At last, two teachers appeared and miraculously pulled us apart, to my unimaginable relief.

We were hauled off to the principal's office and expelled for several days. But when I returned, I was now the kid who had stood toe to toe with Connie Sheehan. My new standing ensured me the right to be left alone by other hoods. The coup de grace was when Connie grinned and wrapped his arm around me, letting it be known that anybody who had a beef with me had to go through him first.

It was in 1951 when we had left the land of the great elm and the meandering Fox River for San Mateo. Three years later when I was thirteen, our family returned to Illinois for a visit.

"You don't know if he's an angel or a devil. If he's real, or not." My cousin Butch, sitting higher up in the tree, regaled me with the strange tale he had just read in a book called *Shane*. Something in me was hooked hard by his intriguing description, and as soon as I could, I found the twenty-five-cent paperback on the drugstore bookstand.

A day later our family began the six-day return drive back home to California, and the slim little book held me all the way across the country. Seated beside my seven-year-old sister Sue, in the back seat of the Hudson, I looked up from my book to see the flat prairieland of Nebraska turning sandy and silvery with sagebrush, as the promise of the West began to appear. We crossed the trickle of the Platte River and got out to look at hundred-year-old wagon ruts preserved in the caked soil. As the open spaces rolled by, the title song from a new wide-screen James Stewart Western, *The Man from Laramie*, poured out from the radio, painting a picture of a lone ride across the plains—my own inner Western.

"He rode into our valley in the summer of '89, a slim man, dressed in black..." (*Shane*, Bantam Books, 1949). Shane deeply imprinted my young adolescence. His mythical presence would follow me through life.

I saved the money from mowing lawns to spend at the nearby stables to ride horses after school. Loping through the golden grasses of the valleys and canyons, free for a time from the alienation and dangers of school, was balm to my spirit. But in 1955, I walked out of murky Borel Junior High into a bright new life at brand new Hillsdale High.

Setting new standards for innovation and excellence, Hillsdale had assembled a crack faculty, won architectural awards, and was featured in *Life Magazine*. Much to our benefit, a couple of the teachers were casualties of the McCarthy scare, recently let go from tainted universities. Talent and intelligence flourished among the students of our little class, many of whom would go on to make a lasting mark on society later in life.

In the warmth and light of new friends, I left behind the chill of Borel. My classmate Elisa Guardino and her gracious mom provided a teenage salon in their home where we could gather. There was Jim Ashford, who built a computer in his garage at the age of sixteen; John Milton, who knew Shakespeare backwards and forwards; adventurous

Jim Woolsey, who would leave school to join the Merchant Marines; Mike Mahan, who would one day become Michael Wingo, an acclaimed painter. Sandy Van Broek, who was comfortable in the labyrinths of James Joyce's *Ulysses*, while the rest of the class cruised through *Johnny Tremain*, would later become a California attorney and lead a ground-breaking, anti-discrimination case for gay rights. Joe Altschule, my improv partner in Drama class, would win an equally historic, precedent-setting victory in the never before used "Battered Spouse Syndrome Defense" to assist victimized and abused women.

There were Friday night and Saturday afternoon drives up to North Beach in San Francisco, where we ordered "expresso" coffee in out of the way cafes. Dressed in our black turtlenecks, with a stray beret or two, we tried to fit in and pass as "beatniks." Not liking the cigarettes that others smoked, I chose a pipe. If nothing else gave away our cover, the sight of a fuzzy-cheeked teenager puffing a pipe accomplished it instantly.

At that time, Lawrence Ferlinghetti, the poet and owner of the famous City Lights Bookstore, could still sometimes be found behind the cash register. He had introduced the idea of making coffee and tea available in the bookstore and providing places to sit and read—a practice later adopted by Barnes & Noble and other booksellers. I loved to wander among the shelves of colorful, beckoning titles.

In gym class one morning, the boys lined up at the trampoline to execute the tumbling exercises coach McGraw was demonstrating. The exercises started out easily enough but grew progressively more difficult, and some of us were having difficulty. The line kept circling back so that we each had to repeat the exercise until we got it right. Repeatedly, amidst titters and guffaws, I fell flat on my face, got up with a self-deprecating laugh, and rejoined the line. By the time I climbed up to the trampoline for the third pass, with hands sweating and stomach churning, I was convinced of only one thing: I couldn't do this. But it was my turn. I did my best, but still I fell once again. There was no laughter this time, only silence. I picked myself up, trying to smile, expecting the usual cutting remarks.

The coach broke the silence, speaking in a voice loud enough for all to hear:

"I'll say one thing, Rich. You sure have a lotta' courage."

How often I have wished I could go back and tell him how much those words meant to me. In that instant, he not only buoyed my sense of self, he gave a group of burgeoning young men a better understanding of "courage."

Back in class, I was urged by the creative writing instructor to enter the "Voice of Democracy" national speech-writing contest. Inspired by my ancestors' involvement in the American Revolution and the Civil War, I felt the blood rise as I composed a fiery essay. It was as if that history was pounding through my veins. My ancestors had signed up to "free the slaves" and "save the union" in 1861; they had fought and died for rights we now take for granted. Instead of a patriotic bromide, the essay was a fresh, challenging take on "democracy." It caught the attention of the judges, and it took first prize for the area school districts. The essay went on to win first prize in the next category, the Bay Area region. It never got farther in the nationals, but the honor was a significant one, and the school principal interrupted class one morning to make the announcement over the loudspeaker. Sitting at my desk, I turned bright red, but smiled inwardly at the public acknowledgement.

Our tall, laconic drama teacher from Colorado, Don Ralston, could read his students like a book and knew how to unseal talent. When I walked to the footlights and stood in the center of a stage to perform for an audience for the first time, I felt a surge of electricity. In that lightning moment I felt at home, more alive than at any time in my life. Mr.

Ralston had cast me in the school play, *The Crucible*, and beaming that electricity out to the audience was as natural and easy as breathing.

Something special had happened that day, and I knew I needed to pay attention to it. Other students were scholars, or sports heroes, or were popular. But now I was home. Riding through the golden hills after school on the big horses of the Borel Stables became less urgent. I could move people! I knew how to act!

It was time to bring *Shane* to drama class. I put together a monologue from the book. "I would see him there in the road, tall and terrible in the moonlight, going down to kill or be killed..." (*Shane*, Houghton Mifflin, 1949; page 118).

In the summer of 1960, following my first year of college, our gang picnicked and played softball in a valley of the golden hills amidst the fragrance of juniper, live-oak, and eucalyptus. In that balmy afternoon, I fell into the smiling blue eyes of a lithe blonde dancer named Jill. At sixteen, she was two years younger than me. A Cree ancestry flowed into her Scandinavian features...a deadly, irresistible beauty.

It was not to be, of course. Two kids intoxicated on the scent of the wild hills could not know that the glow enveloping them was, in reality, just light on their paths of becoming.

"He was the man who rode into our little valley out of the heart of the great glowing West and when his work was done rode back whence he had come and he was Shane" (*Shane*, page 119).

Lost, unable to study, sleep deprived, I spilled my epic tale of love to the college counselor at San Francisco State. He listened silently, sighed, and observed almost wistfully, "I wish I could feel that deeply."

His words were a revelation, opening me to a deeper appreciation of my place in life. They would illumine my journey along the rivers and through the golden hills of the years to come.

CHAPTER 3:
THE OPEN ROAD

You will always be wealthy if you count your riches, as I do, in adventures,
full of life-changing experiences.

—Sam Fuller, *A Third Face – My Tale of Writing,*
Fighting, and Filmmaking

"I'll stick my thumb out and see what happens."

That was what I told myself as I hefted my knapsack over my shoulder and began walking along the open road—the declaration of an eighteen-year-old setting out into the world.

Almost every summer during my four years at San Francisco State, I'd make a lackluster show of looking for a job. Then after a few days I'd take off toward the vast spaces of the American West, just over the Sierra Nevada mountains. I had grown up on Western movies and the myths and legends of the West, and I wasn't about to miss the chance to live those movies and walk through those myths. I wanted to see, sense, smell, and taste the West, to step down from the big screen into real-life adventures of my own.

Setting out, I had no idea where my next meal was coming from or where I would sleep that night, and I wasn't even all that certain about a destination. Curious, open, and game, I wanted to try my luck and just "see what happens."

Those summer treks took me on the highways and back roads of Nevada, Utah, Wyoming, Montana, the Dakotas, Idaho, Colorado, New Mexico, Arizona, Texas—and, once, further east to Michigan to look up a girl from high school. There were truck-stop breakfasts for fifty cents, and nights sleeping under mountain stars or among mosquitoes along the Mississippi. Once, while speeding through the barren stretches of Nevada's red sandstone hills, the New York driver who had given me a ride threw up his hands and exclaimed, "There's nothin' here!" To which I mumbled, "That's why I like it!" Which pretty well summed up my attraction to the West.

Down and out in a Tucson flop house, I had been getting by on one, sometimes two, small meals a day. I put a quarter into the concession machine for a candy bar dinner that night. Worn out from pounding the pavement for work, I gratefully turned out the light. Moments later, I sprang bolt upright when I heard an eruption of scratching and rustling on the walls. Flipping on the light revealed an army of desert-sized roaches, spiders, and centipedes emerging in the coolness for their nightly foray. I learned to sleep with the lights on.

The next day at the employment office, I took work for a week as a landscaper's assistant, providing me enough cash to move on.

I wandered the streets of fabled Tombstone, Arizona, saw the OK Corral, Boot Hill—"Here lies Lester Moore, 4 slugs from a 44, no less, no more"— and the haunts of the Earps, Doc Holliday, Curly Bill, and John Ringo. Standing under the desert sun on the Hoover Dam, with cars whizzing by and my canteen almost out of water, I was close to fainting by the time a ride pulled over.

The Black Hills had lingered in my memory since that long-ago family vacation, and now I found my way back there. The mystical, hazy beauty of that land cast its spell once again, calling me to stay on. In the stillness of a mountain meadow, buffalo munched their way through the tall blue grasses, and white clouds scudded across peaks dark with pine forests. That this was hallowed country for the Sioux was not hard to understand.

In Montana, walking slowly through the rolling hills and worn headstones of the Little Big Horn, I could see Custer and his men going down under Crazy Horse. Later, I found myself in a circle hand in hand with the tall, shy, beautiful girls and boys and men and women of the Northern Cheyenne. I had unknowingly wandered onto the road to their reservation when, luckily for me, the Salvation Army driver en route to his monthly delivery spotted me and screeched to a halt.

"Don't you know where you are!" he hissed.

"Not really."

"You're on the Cheyenne Reservation! Strictly forbidden. Get in!"

And so unfolded an afternoon out of time and space among a people I had long admired but never dreamed I'd spend hours with. Their laughter, their quiet curiosity, and the soft, magical sounds of their language will always be with me. As it turned out, these were descendants of the band of Cheyenne that had joined their Sioux cousins that June day in 1876 to punish Long Hair at Little Big Horn.

Through the ride across Montana, the kindly, sun-bronzed rancher spoke little. Mile after mile, the sea of grass swept out to snow-crowned peaks in the distance. Breaking the silence, I asked, "How many head have you got?"

"Head a' what?" he muttered, keeping his eyes fixed on the highway as it disappeared into distant blue mountains.

"Cattle," I ventured.

"Few hundred," he replied. "But sheep is what we mostly have."

"Oh? How many of them?"

"Fifty, sixty thousand...."

Leaving my ride at Big Timber, I expressed a hope to return one day and live in Montana, the most beautiful country I had ever seen.

"Don't worry, boy. Montana'll always be here."

On the outskirts of Las Vegas, an unshaven exec in rumpled suit and skewed necktie pulled up in his car to ask if I could pay for gas in exchange for a lift. He'd lost everything in the casinos, a sobering glimpse at the underbelly of Vegas glitz.

One summer night, while riding through the rolling plains of eastern Colorado, I am dropped off on an empty road. The prospect of catching another ride looks slim, as cars only appear every five or ten minutes. Down at the crossroads a mile below, there's a gas station and general store, the screen door banging in the soft desert breeze. The western sky is thick with stars, and it's so quiet you can hear for miles. Suddenly, the screen door slams, and a man's gravelly voice is carried on the wind, his whole life captured in one sentence.

"Merle," he exclaims, "ever' time you hit that bed, you go to sleep!"

Maugham or Hemingway could have built a novel from that plea in the night.

I returned home to find a letter from Hawaii. My high school friend Elisa, who had moved to Honolulu with her mother, had invited me for a visit.

Since childhood, the islands had glowed in my heart—almost as if I had once been there. Perhaps it was the memory of a past life, but I longed for the islands as if they were home. Never had my savings been put to better use than when I bought a plane ticket to Hawaii.

When the ramp was lowered and we stepped into that fragrant, balmy air, a line of hula girls waited on the tarmac, singing "Aloha Oe." They kissed us on the cheek, and gently placed leis over our heads and around our shoulders, the age-old welcome to Hawaii. The magic had begun.

At that time, 1962, the long crescent of Waikiki beach was open to the sky, not lined with hotels. That pristine stretch of sand and sea was interrupted only by the Royal Hawaiian, the Moana Surfrider, and the Outrigger—elegant souvenirs of days gone by. Lying on the sand you could still look up and see an unobstructed horizon of dark green mountains against a startling blue sky. Drifting trade winds kept you cool as you sank into the scent of orchids and ginger. You'd swim through the warm, rolling surf, then stretch out under the sun, while beach boys passed by dragging Outrigger canoes, looking for riders.

I stayed in the lanai behind Elisa's house. With each passing day it became more difficult to think about leaving. I missed late registration at San Francisco State. Then I "lost" my plane ticket. Postponing the return flight day after day, I almost missed final registration. Nearly inconsolable, I finally managed to get on a plane. I landed in San Francisco on a cold, foggy day in September, just in time to join the students in line for final registration, a sun-blackened anomaly in a flowered shirt.

In the chilly city, I sought out albums of Hawaiian and South Seas music and played them as I went to sleep. I sang lilting Hawaiian songs and listened on the radio to *Hawaii Calls* on Saturdays. I wept as I watched *The Bird of Paradise* with Debra Paget and Jeff Chandler on my twelve-inch, black and white TV.

I didn't know how or when, I only knew that one day I would return to Hawaii. Many years later, I would honor that promise.

Needing part-time work to help with college costs that fall, I found the perfect job at the San Francisco Zoo driving the Elephant Train tours. I got to be up close with the animals, and during the thirty-minute trip around the zoo, I gave a running monologue, mixed with partially successful attempts at comedy.

Foolishly, the zoo had placed two newly caught Alaskan timber wolves near the entrance in a long, narrow, open cage that provided no natural cover. Crowds pressed close to the cage, and the wolves paced nervously back and forth, feeling vulnerable and unprotected. Within a few days, the wolves grew more and more agitated and became unpredictable. Since the animals were becoming potentially dangerous, the staff removed the cage and relocated the wolves to a meadow in back of the zoo. At the end of each day, as I drove the train back to its garage, I would pass their meadow. Employees were told that the wolves were "intractably vicious and dangerous" animals, and we were warned to stay away from them. I would occasionally see one of the staff catapulting hunks of raw meat into the enclosure from a comfortable distance, muttering curses.

I can't say I paid serious attention to the admonitions to stay away. One day, as my train chugged close to their enclosure, I looked around to make sure no one was in sight. Then I cut the engine, jumped down, and walked over to the enclosure. The wolves stopped in their tracks, with their ears straight up, and watched me approach with their alert amber eyes. They didn't move as I came up to the wire fence, assessing whether I was a threat. When I tossed them scraps from my leftover baloney sandwich, they ignored me and pounced on the food.

The next day as my train rounded the curve and the wolves came in sight, they began to pace up and down, never taking their eyes off me as I approached. This time I threw my leftovers in handfuls, one after another, making sure they saw the deliberateness of the process. On the third day as my train rounded the bend, they began to dash about in anticipation, and when I got out and walked over to the fence, they came right up to me. As I looked into those clear eyes, all separateness dissolved.

I held out the bread and began to push it gingerly through the space in the wire, careful to keep my hand on my side of the fence. They took the food out of my hand and looked at me, blinking, their tongues hanging out. Making friends with these wild, beautiful creatures was a thrill like no other.

On the fourth day, the wolves dashed about as the train approached, and before I pushed the food through the fence, they went down on their front paws in "play mode."

So much for "intractable viciousness." Kindness prevailed.

Some days later, the wolves were gone. I never learned where they were taken or what their fate was. Six months later, the zoo cut back its staff, and I was gone, too.

But before that, there was the "Peaches of Wrath" episode. For me and my pal Sandy, picking fruit sounded like a happy-go-lucky experience we somehow needed to have. So, we hitchhiked to the valleys north of San Francisco, and then headed up the back roads of the orchard country. We quickly found work. The foreman handed us baskets, pointed to the grove of trees and the chattering families among them, and told us to get busy.

We started off in high spirits, joking and singing pop tunes. But as we became entangled in branches and the thorns began to do their work, our breathing grew labored, and our singing faded. Needless to say, the results in our baskets were pitiful compared to those of our fast-picking, expert co-workers. The boss handed us a couple dollars each for our efforts, with words of encouragement that we'd "get better."

Wolfing down our Dinty Moore stew at nightfall with the families around the fire, we became more aware of who we were working with. We began to really see them. Lean, sun-burnt and proud, in well-worn but clean clothes, they were our quiet, shy, smiling tutors. With a twinkle in their eyes, they were helpful and kind to two green kids clearly out of their element. They were a vanishing breed, itinerant American farm workers, who moved from region to region, depending on the season and the crop. They took in stride the company shacks that were provided at each of the picking grounds, expecting only chow and fair payment in exchange for a day of brutal work. When the trees, vines, or bushes were picked clean, they moved on, as easily as the wind.

When we arrived fresh and eager that morning, we'd been ready to throw in our lot, but by the evening, and many bruises and scratches later, we'd had an education. The next morning, after a night sneezing on the straw mattresses in our shack, we bid a melancholy goodbye to the families standing silently. Sobered and humbled by our time among them, scarred by the peaches of wrath, we turned to take the road back to softer ways. And so ended our notions of the romantic, carefree life of fruit pickers.

I had trusted life. I had seen "what happens." I had followed the open road, and it had led me through open doors. More than "living the West," I had experienced a diversity of adventures that would be forever engraved in my memory. Whether easy or difficult, I was the better for every experience. Like Sam Fuller, I was on the road to becoming a wealthy man.

CHAPTER 4:
ARIZONA

It was the summer of 1963. I had finished at San Francisco State, graduating with a B.A. in the nebulous "general social sciences." I had not declared a minor, a strategy that had freed me to explore a wide range of classes in the humanities—literature, history, philosophy, political science, psychology, and anthropology.

I had graduated, but I had also broken up with my girlfriend. My motor scooter had burned out on a trip down the coastal highway to see her in Ventura. I had lost my job as tour guide on the Elephant Train at the San Francisco Zoo. In short, my back was up against the wall. I had mastered no particular skills, had only a few dollars, and zero prospects as I approached my twenty-second birthday. The French Foreign Legion beckoned. I fell back on the one thing I had always done in the past—hit the road.

I decided to use this opportunity to fulfill a life-long dream of working on a ranch. Arizona looked promising, and as I perused the map, I noted promising-looking back roads that might lead into cattle country and the prospect of ranch work. I calculated how long it would take me to hitchhike there, how long my money might last, and assembled my backpack. I figured that I had enough cash to last about three days, barely enough to get to my destination and find work. Once again, I was gambling on my luck.

I said goodbye to my San Francisco apartment and a few friends and set off for northern Arizona. In my trek to West Texas to see the land of Pecos Bill the previous summer, I had picked up a fringed buckskin jacket. I had begun wearing it around San Francisco, despite the occasional taunt or guffaw. Together with the cowboy hat I'd acquired, my getup on this trip preceded the hippies by a couple of years. A friend from San Francisco later wrote to me, "You were the first hippie!"

My gamble bore out. Just three days after catching my first ride out of San Francisco, I arrived at dusk in the village of Alpine, Arizona, high in the White Mountains, the old stronghold of the great Apache chief, Cochise. At the end of the one street was a feed store and what appeared to be an employment booth. I walked over to it.

"Nope, sorry son, no work."

Turning to leave, I noticed a sizable fellow with a toothpick in the corner of his mouth and a wide-brimmed hat over his eyes lounging at the end of the counter. By now it was past sundown, and as I walked down the darkening road, not knowing where I was going, where I would spend the night or what would become of my prospects, a car slowly pulled up alongside of me. I recognized the guy at the wheel—he'd been standing at the end of the counter.

"You lookin' for work?"

"Yeah!" I yelped. He opened the side door and I leaped in, gasping in astonishment at the last-second luck. He said his name was Terry, and that he was building a house at his ranch and needed help.

"What kind of work can you do?"

"I can do general labor. I can hold my own."

"Good enough for me."

Once again, fortune had smiled, and my immediate future seemed assured.

He dropped me at the crossroads gas station/country store where there was a room upstairs for me to flop in for the night.

The next morning, in the cold mountain darkness, he swung by to pick me up and take me to his place for breakfast and to meet the crew. My co-workers were standing around the kitchen table when I walked in with Terry: a red-faced, gruff-voiced, unsmiling middle-aged foreman from Boston; a nineteen-year-old kid, gung-ho to join the Special Forces who would drive the tractor; and an old, beat-up ex-cowboy and rodeo rider who would become my buddy. The woman of the house stood over an immense round pot on the stove and commenced throwing huge chunks of ground beef, tomatoes, potatoes, and onions into a sizzling mound that would be our breakfast, washed down with black coffee. Then we strode out into the clean, mountain morning air, piled in the car, and drove the short distance to the site.

The ex-cowpoke and I were assigned the job of hauling small boulders down from the mountainside in a wheelbarrow, digging the foundation, and then filling it in with our harvest off the mountain. By midday the sun was brutally hot, and we worked shirtless, constantly thirsty, taking shallow breaths at 7,000 feet. It was without doubt the hardest work I'd ever done. Hands on hips and scowling, the foreman shouted unflattering remarks about our efforts. I began to build up a strong desire to get the hell out of there, once I'd saved up my wages.

When we'd break for lunch, I'd stride into the diner, ravenous, and order an enormous burger with all the trimmings. Even after that cowboy breakfast, you needed another heaping plate of fuel to get you through the afternoon.

The old rodeo rider lived with his Indian wife in a sheet-metal shack on the side of the mountain. At one of our breaks, he taught me how to roll a cigarette with one hand; a skill I would never utilize but appreciated all the same. He walked with a limp, and it was plain to see that the brutal work was taking a toll on him.

"How'd you get hurt?" I asked him. "What's the story?"

"Horse rolled on me," he mused, squinting through the tobacco smoke. "So I pulled my .45 and shot that son of a bitch."

I woke up one Saturday morning violently ill, vomiting and feverish. Alone in my room over the gas station, I wondered how I'd get well, let alone rouse myself to go to work with the gang on Monday morning. Right on schedule, shortly after dawn two days later, the car pulled up, our foreman in the driver's seat. Still feeling weak and feverish, I staggered to the door, croaking to the foreman that I was sick and couldn't join them.

"That's a load of crap!" he bellowed. "Get in the car! We'll sweat it out of ya'!"

Stunned, I staggered back inside and managed to crawl into my clothes and walk unsteadily out to the car. Somehow, though weak, without breakfast, and cowed by the boss, I found myself feebly hauling rocks down the mountain once again. At first, I struggled, sweating profusely, but slowly I grew steadier on my feet. A few hours later my fever was gone, and I was feeling strong. By lunchtime I was 100% myself! I hated to admit it, but that damned foreman was onto something. "Hard-luck" medicine.

Regardless of the beauty of the White Mountains, and my respect for Terry and the fair wage I was making, by the end of three weeks I'd had enough. I announced that I would be moving on. I decided to head to Las Vegas to see my uncles, my mother's brothers, Johnny and George

Dallas; two bachelor WW2 vets who had been through the hell of the South Pacific and now were content to work peaceably and uneventfully at the post office. Like most vets of that time, they never spoke of the war, and spent their subsequent years reclusively and in quiet acts of kindness for others. In my four or five days with them, they taught me how to play keno, and I won some much-needed traveling money.

I heard that the Army would soon be in touch for my required physical, and I knew my traveling days were numbered. So, in early fall I headed back to the family home in California.

At the house, I saw old friends and took my Army physical. I made the decision to enlist so as to have a choice in job assignments and not wind up in some godforsaken post in Georgia or Alabama. I went in on November 12, 1963, when the world seemed relatively sane. John F. Kennedy was President, and the risk of war seemed low. Ten days later the world turned upside down when the president was shot by an assassin.

CHAPTER 5:
THE MOVEABLE FEAST

*If you are lucky enough to have lived in Paris as a young man, then wher-
ever you go for the rest of your life, it stays with you, for Paris is a mov-
able feast.*

—ERNEST HEMINGWAY TO A FRIEND, 1956

Bundled up in jacket and scarf, I trudged through the December snow
across the Petit Pont to Shakespeare and Company, on the other side of
the river opposite Notre Dame. Inside the bookstore, I greeted George,
the goateed proprietor, pawed through the new releases, and looked at
the latest *New York Herald*. Then I poured myself a glass of cider at a table
by the door and found my way up the familiar stairs. The bookstore was
a favorite rendezvous of Hemingway, Fitzgerald, Gertrude Stein, Ezra
Pound, and other expatriate writers during the 1920s. Shakespeare and
Company was my home away from home while stationed in Paris in the
mid-1960s.

Past the shelves of books and the occasional cots where wayfarers
could pass a night or two, a pretty, dark-haired woman of about forty in a
stewardess uniform was perusing titles. She smiled, and recognizing that

we were both American, we laughed and struck up a conversation about how much we loved this place. I mentioned that I'd begun writing a poem while on a troopship a year earlier. She expressed an interest, and in the months to come, whenever we encountered each other at Shakespeare & Company, I would show her new pieces that I'd written. In her encouragement, she became like a patron.

Caroline was her name.

"Do you know Monsieur Guy?" she asked.

I replied that I didn't, which surprised her, given that most artistic types in Paris knew of Monsieur Guy. I was hardly a carefree artist, however, but a soldier at United States European Command Headquarters, stationed just outside of Paris at the garrison in Saint-Germain-en-Laye.

"Let me tell you about Monsieur Guy. He has an apartment in the Arab quarter that he lets people use from time to time. I have a key, and I can pass it on to you. That's how it works. That's how M. Guy wants to share his place, with whomever needs it at the time."

"M. Guy is a communist, of course."

A *real* communist, he believed in sharing his goods freely. At this time, 1965, the United States was locked in a Cold War with the Soviet Union. For a twenty-three-year-old soldier stationed at one of the most sensitive posts in the American military, associating with a communist could result in unpleasant consequences. Even a pure communist like M. guy, someone with good intentions, not involved in political intrigue, was still officially an "enemy." With that chilling thought in my mind, I very gingerly accepted Caroline's key to M. Guy's apartment. Whenever I left the post on a weekend pass to go to Paris and stay at the apartment, I would turn to see if I was being followed.

Once freed from the gray, soulless barracks, my heart rose and my step quickened as I wandered through the Latin Quarter, seeking a hidden bistro for dinner. Just off an avenue, on an ancient, winding street barely wide enough for a car, the lamplight of a small café spilled into the lane, inviting passersby in for an evening meal. I would find myself at a small candle-lit table close beside a couple who smiled and bid me, "Bonsoir." I would order the menu du jour, or "steak pommes frites" and a salade vert, with a glass of vin rouge ordinaire. Brie or camembert and sliced pear was served for dessert, followed by a café espress. Afterwards, I'd slide back my chair and light a pipe. In the curling smoke, I fell into warmth and candlelight and soft chatter and lost myself on the Left Bank.

When John Ford's classic 1956 film, *The Searchers,* was revived with French subtitles at the big theatre on the Champs Elysees, I stood in quiet anticipation with families and students in a line stretching down the street. I had been swept up by the film, extolling its greatness since I saw it the first time, but years passed before critics did the same. To experience it now through French eyes was deeply gratifying. "Oh, c'est beau...!"

You would think that GIs lucky enough to be stationed just outside of Paris would flock to the city any chance they got, but the bus from the base was usually sparsely filled. It was sobering to learn that many of them had only a casual interest in Paris and the French way of life. More than once during my years in Paris I was bemused to hear, "I can't get a decent hamburger down there."

Paris was my haven and my playground. Its iconic buildings, low to the horizon, let in plenty of sky. It was easy to pass hours in the snug cafes of its tree-lined avenues. If you felt the urge to capture a thought, waiters were quick to bring paper and pencil. For years, writers had frequented the cafes, and the request was a familiar one. Young adventurers like Hemingway, feeling an inspiration, would call for paper and pencil, creating masterpieces on café tables in the afternoon sun.

The U.S. Army was fighting in Vietnam, yet here I was, safe, in the most enchanting city in the world. How did that happen?

In the fall of 1964, I sat at my desk, fearing that at any moment my sanity might give way, and I would do something stupid. In my first posting after boot camp, I had been assigned to the 94th Evacuation Hospital at Fort Lewis, Washington; specifically, to learn the job of a clerk who was soon to be mustered out. The khaki uniform I wore barely contained the forces swirling beneath it. I was about to explode from the tedium, regimentation, and sterility of military life. I had to find a way out.

In desperation, I pored through the Army's book of regulations, frantic for a glimmer of hope. There, in a chapter titled "Transfers," I came across a wildly unlikely possibility. "A transfer may be requested if there is more than one individual in the same position." My breath quickened and my eyes widened. Of course! There was still a guy in the position I was training for. I was only there in order to learn his job so that I could replace him in two months! Wouldn't that situation be obvious?

There was just a chance. Why not take the gamble? I had nothing to lose and everything to gain. I bet on the military mentality; that they wouldn't see outside the box.

I meticulously typed up the paperwork, citing the appropriate regulation number, and with pounding heart, I got up and walked into the office of the Lieutenant to submit my request for transfer to Europe. I held my breath as I watched him slowly read through the papers. I could almost see his mind working: *Yes, there's the regulation number, alright, and yes, that seems to be so, that there's more than one person for the same job.* I could hardly believe it when I saw him sign his name, grab the stamp, and slam it down, "Approved!"

From his office the paperwork went across the hall to his superior, the Captain, who perused it peremptorily, saw that his Lieutenant had signed it, and without hesitation, stamped it with his approval. When he, in turn, submitted it to the Major down the hall, the Major followed the same sequence. Seeing that the paperwork looked proper and that both his subordinates had approved it, the Major did likewise; then he submitted it through channels to Washington. Final word would take weeks.

Tensely, I watched the mail come in day after day. Surely, the Pentagon would discover the flaw in the request. At last we received the paperwork, and without so much as a raised eyebrow, I was issued orders for transfer to a post in Germany, and from there, to Paris!

The lesson burned into my brain. Keep taking chances! And never be afraid to think outside the box.

As I shouldered my duffel bag and walked across the Fort Lewis parking lot for the last time, the Major was walking from the opposite direction. We saluted in passing, and he remarked gruffly under his breath, "I wish I was goin' with ya."

Herded into a troopship, I set out across the North Atlantic with hundreds of other soldiers. I was grateful to be assigned "guard duty" on the upper deck from midnight to four in the morning. Alone in the wind, the silence was broken only by the slosh of waves against the hull, as the bow rose and fell against a black sky alive with stars. In those mystical hours in the vast ocean night, lines of poetry began to form.

A few days later a storm began to blow, and we were ordered to stay below deck. I knew seasickness would be my fate if I were crammed into the hold with hundreds of others while the ship heaved over hills and valleys of waves. Amidst the confusion of troopers scurrying down ladders to the berths below, I snuck back up on deck, wrapped myself around a post, and prepared to ride out the storm. Instead of making me ill, the cold wind and pelting rain were a tonic, and I held on as the ship slid slowly down walls of water and up and out again. I was one with the heaving Atlantic, laughing in the roaring wind, the rain stinging my face—in awe.

When the train pulled into Paris on New Year's Eve in 1965, I changed into civilian clothes in the station, and breathless with excitement, I started walking. I had no idea where I was in the city, only that I was at last in "The City of Light," about to begin the adventure of a lifetime. It was a dream come true, and I wanted to drink it all in, street by street. I walked for hours, tasting her haunts and dives. By the time dawn broke, the vague sketch of Paris from my youthful imaginings had become real. In a glow, I entered the Army base at Saint-Germain-en-Laye just as the sun was coming up.

During those first months I became friends with a tall PFC named Brent. An inspired poet, lady's man, and inveterate pot smoker, Brent was prone to falling into trouble. Long after curfew, he would amble into the barracks from a rendezvous at some smoky cellar jazz club on the Left Bank, laughing and incoherently slurring lines of poetry. Fortunately for him, his father was the Colonel in command of the base. He had arranged for Brent to be assigned there so that he could keep his eye on him.

In the fall of 1965, President Johnson sent one hundred thousand marines and soldiers to Vietnam, and the world shifted as the U.S. entered a major war. The Colonel would successfully protect Brent from being transferred there, but I heard that my former outfit from Fort Lewis, the 94th Evacuation Hospital, was en route to the jungles. Because something had nudged me to take a wild chance on an obscure Army regulation a year earlier, I would not be crawling through a rice paddy in Vietnam. I was in Paris.

The sense of being taken care of was not new to me. I had felt it at various other times in my life.

The couple that had sat at the back of my world literature class at San Francisco State during the fall semester of 1962 was a few years older. The woman had long, flowing brown hair, a gentle smile, and wore a cape. He wore a wide-brimmed hat, boots, and sported a sweeping mustache. In their dress and manner, they looked like the hippies that would appear across America a few years later. I sometimes caught them regarding me, and when our eyes met and they smiled, something deep within was touched.

Roaming the West the previous summer, I had brought along *The Brothers Karamazov*. It was a reading assignment for the upcoming class. Fireworks exploded in my brain when I read Dostoevsky's novel, as if he was speaking directly to me. Finally, someone had captured how life really was! I could hardly wait to dive headlong into its depths in class.

As I leaned forward at my desk, my whole being alert to the professor's opening remarks, Mr. Gerard smiled, straightened his bow tie, cleared his throat, and declared, "Now, I think we all understand that this isn't the way life really is...."

I quickly sank back in my seat, face flushed, ears ringing. I glanced at the other students, their eyes lusterless, nodding quietly in agreement. It was another pivotal moment, akin to hearing the school psychologist tell me he wished he could feel as deeply as I did. I was face to face with the fact that my experience of life was not like that of others—at least, not in that class. It seemed as if my passion for the Karamazovs was unacceptable. About to jump in and respond with wild enthusiasm, I had been saved from embarrassment in the nick of time. Stunned and baffled, but a little wiser, I remained silent throughout the remaining discussions on *The Brothers Karamazov*. The couple in cape and wide-brimmed hat in the back of the class, clearly friends of the Karamazovs, smiled knowingly.

Later in the semester I found myself in the aisle of the library, enthralled by a book called *Summerhill*, which chronicled a new and revolutionary way of relating to children. I looked up to see the couple, a few paces away, smile as if to say, *You're on the right track*. I was too shy to open a conversation with them, but I'll never forgot their benevolent presence in my life. They were like emissaries from the future, harbingers of a time to come, gently guiding a fledgling explorer. I wish I had been able to break through my reserve and approach them. If I could go back through time and space, I would tell them how much those fleeting encounters had meant in my life.

Sylvia made her mark as well, a girl who came to San Francisco State from the woods of northern California. Duke University had engaged her for experiments with ESP and discovered that, among her other abilities with psi phenomena, she could see colors not on the spectrum. As serene and composed as a Buddha, Sylvia was soft-spoken and beautiful, with flowing auburn hair. She introduced me to the healing, penetrating verses of Kahlil Gibran's *The Prophet* and Lao Tzu's window into the universe, *The Way of the Tao,* books that opened me to a wondrous, mystical knowledge of life that she knew I somehow sensed but wasn't consciously aware of.

Guides, seen and unseen, had always been there marking the path, and now I was in Paris, far from the flaming carnage of Vietnam. From one "city of light," as we called San Francisco, I was now in another.

Sometime in 1966, Brent and I heard about LSD. The Beatles were experimenting with it, and Timothy Leary, a professor at Harvard, was espousing psychedelic drugs as a way of opening doors into worlds beyond our immediate awareness. I paid special attention to something Leary emphasized in his writings. He said it was important to confront your fears and clear them up before using LSD, and then you should have no problems with it. Apparently, those who blindly used it without first cleaning up their minds would have to deal with the consequences of whatever problems they hadn't resolved.

It was a caution I duly noted, then abruptly threw to the wind; we would make plans to try LSD at the earliest opportunity. Brent would buy it from one of his many contacts in Paris, and we would figure it out from there. We heard that his dad would be away for a week, leaving his chateau vacant. Naturally, we would choose to experiment with LSD at the home of the base commander.

When the momentous Saturday arrived, we took the train to his dad's imposing, empty chateau outside Saint-Germain-en-Laye. Not knowing what to expect, we spent a few breathless minutes reassuring each other that we would stay close together, safely contained within the walls of the chateau, and that under no circumstances would we venture outside—or, the height of stupidity, would we go to Paris!

Within moments of ingesting the strips of LSD, all previous plans flew out the window. Laughing for no apparent reason, we stared at each other for a second, then simultaneously blurted out, "Let's go to Paris!" All the way into town on the metro ride, we stood in the aisle hanging onto the pole, taking in the world as if for the first time. Like a couple of six-year-olds, we traded glances and broke into innocent bursts of laughter.

We emerged from the metro at Place Saint Michel on the Left Bank, our usual stomping grounds. By now the LSD was in full effect. I became fixated on the people passing by, and I was astonished to find myself spouting specific insights about each one of them. It was as if latent intuitive powers had been ignited. Insights that normally we are only dimly conscious of, if at all, were now at the forefront. I swiftly identified essential traits in people in the space of a mini-second. The passersby became too numerous for me to keep up with my running list of details. I sat down on the curb and carried on my rapid-fire monologue describing the feelings and personal traits of as many people passing by on the boulevard as I could.

This went on for most of the night, until Brent and I started feeling hungry. We were the earliest breakfast customers at the nearby café. As the LSD faded, I remember proclaiming, "All Americans should have some of this in their morning coffee every day!" Based on the revelations I'd experienced throughout the night it seemed clear to me that a little LSD to start the day would go a long way in straightening out our country.

CHAPTER 6:
LE PAPILLON BLEU

I hadn't been in the barracks for more than a year when it was announced that there was a problem with overcrowding.

"I know this is gonna' be hard," the Captain told the assembled company, "but we need to ask for a few volunteers to live off-base. You'll of course retain all the amenities of being able to take your chow in the mess hall, use the PX, or any of the other base privileges, and we'll reimburse your trips to and from work, if that's an issue. Any questions?"

My heart thumping, I shot up my hand almost before he was finished.

My new quarters were at Le Papillon Bleu, the Blue Butterfly, a small, centuries old inn with four guest rooms in the forest adjacent to the base. It happened to be the forest of Saint-Germain-en-Laye, where Henri de Navarre, King of France in the 16th century, used to hunt stag and wild boar. A little upstairs room at the end of a short hallway would be my home for the next two years. Among other claims to fame, the inn was renowned for having the best fondue in northern France. Luck continued to smile.

Every morning, I would walk down a path through the forest to the gates of the base, while the mist rose and dew sparkled on the leaves. I would usually pack a book with me, and maybe a bit of cheese and bread from breakfast at the inn, so that at lunch, or on the way home in the afternoon, I could stop a while under my favorite oak to read, bask in nature, and collect myself after the discord of my Army day.

While finishing up at San Francisco State, many books had called to me that I wouldn't get to read in my remaining time there. I started writing down titles, and by the time I went into the army, I had accumulated a list of about eighty books. In the cold, lifeless stations of army life, books were a haven. They were my teachers and companions. Drawing on my pipe in the post library of an evening, a copy of *Look Homeward, Angel* or *The Razor's Edge* or *For Whom the Bell Tolls* in hand, I warmed again to adventure, to the open road, to the eternal truths. I found peace in those pages and felt again the glow of life. Sometimes, drifting in the pipe smoke, lines of my own began to form.

My objective was to make my way through my list of books, continuing college, so to speak, while in the army. I didn't anticipate how the books would, in turn, lead me to still more titles. Even though the list kept growing, I read most of them by the end of my four years.

Brent was strolling along the path one afternoon when he discovered me, propped up against the oak, engrossed in my book. "What're you reading?" I put down my pipe and showed him the cover, *War and Peace.* He burst into laughter. The irony that we were in an army currently in a war raging in Vietnam was delicious.

That was not the only moment of irony I was to have at the base, and far less harrowing than others.

It was because of the Army Special Services that I returned to performing after having abandoned it at San Francisco State. There, at college, I had been put off by the coldness of the theatre world and froze up as an actor. Now, several years later, I found the atmosphere of amateur theatre in the military warm and welcoming.

United States European Command Headquarters was the American military wing of NATO and it was comprised of more generals, admirals, and senior officers than any other American post in the world. Officers outnumbered enlisted men and women, and we had an audience of hundreds for our performances of *Gallows Humor, Twelve Angry Men, Born Yesterday, Lily, The Felon's Daughter*—and the coup de grace, *Visit to a Small Planet*. Gore Vidal's biting satire of the military was hilarious. Did we dare present this glaringly anti-war farce before rows of senior officers on one of the most powerful bases in the world? Surely, it could result in serious reprimand, or punitive action.

In the lead role as Kreton, the wayward visitor from the stars who romps merrily and irreverently through the military, with many a quip that could turn a general or admiral red with righteous rage, I prepared for opening night with apprehension. I would be the chief target for the umbrage the play was sure to arouse.

When the curtain went up on our wicked little comedy, we held our breath as one outrageous, provocative line after another shot out from the stage. Stunned silence fell on the rows of beribboned uniforms. Then, suddenly, the silence was ripped by roaring guffaws and knee slapping. Of course! Who would appreciate dark, anti-war humor more than veterans! As the curtain came down, instead of court martials, we received a standing ovation.

In the sterility of that world, you could suddenly be surprised, even in the darker hours. You never knew what genius might be concealed beneath the uniform of a PFC. I would laugh for years at the quip some unknown trooper in the ranks mumbled as we stood silently at reveille one morning. "And the meek shall inhibit the earth."

My wise friend Caroline, from Shakespeare & Company, who had led me to M. Guy and the apartment in the Arab quarter, gifted me again when she introduced me to a warm and gracious Rumanian family, the Axels, former aristocrats who had fled the dictatorial communist nation and were now living on the Right Bank. I became good friends with the brother and sister, Mickey and Colette, and they began inviting me to Sunday dinners with the family. They were eager to know about all things American and wanted to hear all about California.

They loved to go to the Cinematheque, the French museum of motion pictures, to see classic American films. Together we relished the powerful, lyrical Western, *The Broken Lance,* from blacklisted director, Edward Dmytryk. We saw Howard Hawks' *The Big Sleep,* Vincente Minnelli's musical masterpiece, *The Band Wagon,* Sam Peckinpah's elegiac, *Ride the High Country,* and the idyllic portrait of a Quaker farm family, *Friendly Persuasion,* perhaps William Wyler's greatest film. One of the most beautiful films of all, George Stevens' breathtaking adaptation of *Shane,* was captured by the American poet Carl Sandburg: "The whole thing seems to be happening at the bottom of a clear deep pool."

It was at the museum that I first heard of "auteur theory," which essentially means that a strong director such as Hawks or John Ford reflects his own values and vision as the "author" or principal creator of the film. By contrast, it's clear that many fine films are more the product of a team than a strong director. Michael Curtiz, for example, who directed such diverse classics as *Casablanca, Yankee Doodle Dandy,* and *White Christmas,* was so versatile and collaborative that you would be hard pressed to find his fingerprint on his films. The museum gave me a fresh view of American movies. I was able to see them anew, through the eyes of Parisian culture, and gained a deeper love and appreciation for American film art.

One Sunday dinner at the Axels, the gathering included a new guest, a quiet woman of about fifty with a long, sad face, a mane of red hair and twinkling green eyes. Her name was Nina Cassian, the Rumanian National Poet, visiting Paris in an official cultural capacity. As we spoke over dinner, her situation became clear. She was not free, even though she was in Paris. Beneath her soft-spoken voice and warm cordiality, there was a sadness. The government of her nation had her locked in a cold grip because of her family in Rumania. The idea of cutting ties with her family and creating a new life of freedom in France was out of the question. I gathered the confidence to mention I was writing something myself, an epic poem of sorts, and her eyes brightened. With the kindness of an accomplished artist, she asked me who my "influence" was as a writer. I thought for a moment, and then I said, "Walt Whitman," which brought a bright smile to her face.

I saw her a couple more times at various gatherings during those weeks, and a gentle bond began to develop between us. Then, suddenly, she was gone. I attempted to reach her by letter to learn if she was alright. I wondered, had her brief friendship with an American soldier jeopardized her in some way? I never heard back from her. I don't know what kind of life she returned to in Rumania, or what became of her, and if the family in Paris knew, they didn't say.

But by now, my days in Paris were drawing to an end. In 1967 De Gaulle kicked the American military out of France. When they asked for volunteers who spoke some French to stay behind to help during the transition, I quickly stepped forward. I stretched out my days in Paris as best I could, until it became obvious that further delay was not possible. I left in April, one of the last American soldiers to do so. On the boulevards, and in the forest of Saint-Germain-en-Laye, the leaves of the trees were a translucent green, just beginning to bud. I said goodbye to Brent, Caroline, and the Axels, the charm of Le Papillon Bleu, M. Guy's hideaway, and the lights of Shakespeare and Company. Then I boarded the train to Stuttgart, Germany, the new headquarters for U.S. European Command, where I would wait out the last few months of my enlistment.

I would be spoiled forever. The French made art out of everyday life. Even the commonest cafés in Paris knew the secrets of fine cuisine, and in subsequent years, my taste buds would wistfully remember. Paris was a glittering way station, a place of becoming that welcomed seekers and wanderers and those who weren't quite defined. I was "lucky enough to have lived in Paris as a young man" and she would smile in me forever.

I had completed the poem I'd begun almost three years earlier. I called it "Out of the West," and sent it to various literary journals and magazines. Looking back at it now, it seems a little self-involved, but it did capture a raw, young spirit rising in defiance.

1.

Out of the heart
Of the West I rode,
Daring you only
To kiss your fears.

I, of the churning blood
And low blue fire,
Shedding collars and ties,
Burning all papier-mache hearts,
And bringing a soul into your eyes.

I come and go
Like a wisp of campfire smoke.
Captives tremble
And dare to kill butterflies.

2.

If you are bold....
Only the sea is vast enough for you,
And you are at home in its boundlessness.

You find peace in the unbridled flux
And see, at last, a true reflection of your
Deepest self in these quiet, bowelless shades.

3.

Like golden silk your hair spilled
Over white shoulders...the
Curve of your dancing azure eyes traced
Your Cree blood.
In glances of naked heat
And smiles soft in adoration
You brought me to myself.

4.

Through these cold, weary hours the fires still
Smolder angrily. I lie dormant.

But I will not forget how to dream,
How to sing and laugh, or how to hate.

And with the Spring, the sun again will warm my back,
The breeze brush my face.

I will walk long in the hip-high meadow grass
And ride a lathered pony
Across a windy, unbound prairie.

5.

To keep going on
To crawl the endless desert,
Remembering
The scent of blue prairie evening
And summer wind in the blackjack trees
To smile and spur the mount

Into every dim canyon
To die
Riding big and free
Across the rim

6.

On and on, always moving, always dreaming
Through the lilac dusk of the mountain valley,
In the dust under copper desert skies...
Always the song of guitars and a tumbleweed
And riders on the rim

7.

There's nothing left but a faint red pulse,
Unadorned by dreams, hopes, ambitions,
Or the naïve, painkilling vision of martyrdom.
Just a speck of will
Against all the forces of Heaven,
To turn death into life

A little listless, perhaps,
Under the ruins of a thousand defeats.

8.

Though I go now . . .

In the sagebrush whispers
Of desert sunset,
Where horsemen ride
against the winter moon,
When the lion
Trots the savannah...
Find me there.

See my reflection
In every child's tears
And hear my laughter in the high mountains
When Man, at last, is free.

During that final summer in the army, a letter arrived from the editor of *Poet Lore*, one of the country's oldest literary publications, whose early volumes had included Walt Whitman and F. Scott Fitzgerald. "Out of The West" would be printed in the next issue! Around that same time, I was accepted to The American Musical & Dramatic Academy in New York, beginning the following year in May of 1968. A bright new life was taking shape.

Every day for four years I had held my breath and hoped my luck would hold in the chilling, alien, autocratic world of the military. In the late fall of 1967, hardly believing I'd made it through, I came to the end of my enlistment. Breathing deeply, I walked away a free man, more whole than before, graced by the soul-deepening days and nights of Paris.

On the base earlier that year I had followed the Six Day War, enthralled by the brilliance, pluck, and daring of the Israeli people. With my heart set on one last overseas adventure, I set out to see that faraway country. I would encounter life-altering times there, on the Gaza Strip.

CHAPTER 7:
ON THE GAZA STRIP

I'd sold my blood to pay for the boat passage to Haifa.

It was nothing new – I had sold blood to get from Greece to Turkey, and from Turkey to Cyprus. But when I went to the blood bank in Cyprus, the doctor had questioned me, per routine, as to whether I had donated recently. I lied at first, afraid they wouldn't take my blood and then I wouldn't have the money to get to Israel. But as he strapped on the contraption, I grew thoughtful.

"Why?" I asked, "Is there some sort of danger?"

"You can develop anemia if you've given more than two times in the past four weeks."

I wasn't at all sure of the timing, but I knew I had no other way to get to my destination. I had underestimated how far my army discharge pay would take me, and now I was strapped for cash. I was dead set on experiencing Israel. "It's alright," I said, "Go ahead."

Landing at Haifa, I walked the short distance down the dock to the Tourist/Kibbutz Information Center. The official looked me over. Seeing that I was an American, he assumed I would prefer an assignment on one of the famous, established kibbutzim in the interior, where most Americans and other foreigners gravitated.

"Have you got something a little more on the frontier? Not so settled, a bit more where the action is?"

He eyed me briefly, then wrote something down on a piece of paper and passed it to me.

"Let's try this. A small outpost on the Gaza Strip, about seventy people, Kibbutz Nir-Am."

"Sounds fine!"

It was early January in 1968, six months after the Six Day War had ended. Before being discharged from United States European Command Headquarters in Stuttgart, Germany, I had followed hourly dispatches as the war unfolded, as riveting to read as a Ken Follet thriller. Since that Monday morning in June 1967, when I was shocked to see the latest report on the ticker tape machine—"Israel at war on 3 fronts"—I had been drawn to the ingenuity and indomitability of these vibrant people.

I had graduated from college without choosing a profession. There was, however, one thing I had excelled at ever since high school—performing in plays. During my time in the service, I had come to realize that I should try to do for a living what I did well. I was thrilled that The American Musical & Dramatic Academy in New York City had accepted me for their two-year training, beginning in May. But before returning to the States, I wanted to walk a while among the people of Israel.

A few days after Christmas, with snow falling quietly all along the way, I boarded a train and traveled from Stuttgart down through Yugoslavia and into Greece, and then sailed to Turkey and Cyprus, finally arriving at the little settlement on the Gaza Strip.

The first morning on the kibbutz I found myself seated at a long table trying in vain to assemble a breakfast amidst reaching, flailing arms, furiously chomping cheeks, and a crescendo of incomprehensible Hebrew. I was saved by the halting English of one of my table mates.

"Here, you better grab some of this, my friend," laughed a sun-bronzed, bewhiskered face in a slouch hat. He passed me a towering bowl of fluffy yogurt, a plate of hard-boiled eggs, and slices of hot bread, all from the kibbutz.

Soon I was in the orchards picking grapefruit with a couple dozen chattering men and women. The pace was pleasant under a warm, morning desert sun. I was asked where I was from, and how long I'd be staying, and what did I think about Vietnam? At lunch, it was the same, gentle free for all at the long table, reaching and gesticulating, and quickly learning how to say, "Pass the potatoes," if I didn't want to go hungry.

In the evening after dinner, people would gather in the social hall. There was no theatre, no television, no films, but plenty of newspapers and books. And in the corner, there was a place where you could serve yourself various teas grown at Nir-Am, and honey from another kibbutz. We could read or socialize—or attempt to socialize, in my case. Then off to bed in the fragrant desert night, rising at dawn to another rousing breakfast and the waiting rows of grapefruit trees.

Not many days had passed before I learned of the man called Yanchik, or "Big Mustache," as the roving Bedouin called him. One of the original pioneers, or sabras, he had been in Israel since before the War of Independence in 1948, and had experienced peaceable, and sometimes not so peaceable, dealings with the roaming tribes. He had learned their ways, just as they in turn had studied him, and a mutual respect and friendship had been born. He was known to hold court in his cabin after supper, so I settled in with a modest crowd as inconspicuously as possible, as the tall, graying sabra with the enormous mustache lit his pipe and laconically began to spin tales. Here before me was the unacknowledged leader of Kibbutz Nir-Am.

In the wee hours of my third or fourth night on the kibbutz, the blast from an explosion on the road outside rolled me out of my cot onto the floor. An intruder of some sort, possibly a guerrilla fighter, had attempted to cross the perimeter and had touched off a landmine. I never learned the full story, and the residents of Nir-Am took it all in stride.

Because of its vulnerable location on the Gaza Strip, this kibbutz had been assigned a detachment of female soldiers to provide additional security. You would not want to make the mistake of underestimating their capabilities, making presumptions based on their gender. As a stranger slowly adapting to the culture and learning the customs of the land, I clumsily flirted with one of the comelier troopers, whose name was Yael. Judging by her puzzled look and blushing cheeks, I don't think she knew what to make of the half-baked advances of this foreigner.

I had thought to bring a thick notebook along with me on this trip. Carrying it with me constantly, I found myself making frequent use of it. I had made friends with several of my co-workers in the orchards and they began to share their stories with me. Without exception, everyone had a tale to tell, and I wrote feverishly to keep up. They were from various countries—Argentina, Morocco, Russia, the Netherlands. Rolling back their sleeves, many of them revealed the row of numbers on their arms. It was a revelation to learn that people had occasionally escaped from the death camps and found their way to Israel. Curled up in garbage barrels, they were rolled onto ships and survived in that state for days until they came to port and climbed out on the shores of Haifa. Their relief was short lived, as many were quickly handed a rifle and found themselves fighting the Arab Legion during the War of Independence.

It was now six months since the harrowing battles of June 1967. As we strolled to the orchards one morning, my Argentinian companion, conscious of my journal, pointed and said:

"Right over there is where we captured a Russian lady general."

"What!" I exclaimed. "Wow! What did you do?"

"We didn't want anything to do with it," he quietly smiled. "We just gave her to the Russians and asked them to leave us alone."

One night, lying in my sleeping bag, I had a nightmare, during which I let out a blood-curdling scream, instantly shocking me awake. As I struggled to stand up, untangling myself from the sleeping bag, Israeli soldiers with submachine guns burst into the hut. Within seconds, they scanned the scene, asked me what happened, nodded quietly, and left. Although mortified, I couldn't fail to notice how calmly the incident had been accepted and understood, and I realized that the terror of nightmares was an all too frequent occurrence here. They saw me as a man fresh from the U.S. Army, probably Vietnam, and that helped to seal their acceptance of me as a fellow veteran of horrific violence. They weren't entirely wrong—I had not been to Vietnam, but I did manage to carry within me the makings for some dandy nightmares.

One Saturday, the Sabbath, when I was free from work for the day, I decided to go into the city of Gaza. I wanted to see for myself a place and a people that the outside world had little knowledge of. At that time there were no restrictions on who could go into Gaza, surprising as that may seem.

It was in those minutes of walking out of the kibbutz on my way to catch the bus that I experienced a profound, life-altering encounter, one of the most spiritually significant of my life.

Passing the garbage dump, I spotted a rat behind the chain-link fence, about eight or ten inches long, eyeing me steadily. Feeling revulsion for a disease carrier, a pest to be avoided or quickly destroyed, is a common instinct for most of us. I was no different. Without a moment's hesitation, and with mounting excitement, I snatched up a rock. The rat sat motionless, watching me. Summoning years of boyhood experience, I threw quickly, and the rat jumped as the rock clattered to the ground, just missing him. Trying to hone in, I hurled another; it landed close to him on the opposite side, and he jumped again. Quickly assessing the gravity of threat that he faced, the rat scampered backwards, and found himself up against the wall of the dumpster. Another rock crashed to his left, then one to his right, as I slowly advanced, closing in . . .

He then did something so extraordinary that it took my breath away, something that would forever shape my understanding of the sacredness of life, and my place in it. Cornered, trapped, with nowhere to escape, seeing his fate, he suddenly stopped moving, turned, and slowly and majestically rose up on his hind legs to face me. Without hope, he stood there defiantly, meeting his fate head on. I stopped cold, my mouth hanging open, stunned. Shamed to my core, I limply tossed my rocks to the side and reverently muttered, "You win, brother."

For a timeless instant, a bright new light illumined my world. I had seen the soul of the rat. He had opened mine.

It was as if a play had been staged to remind me of the beauty and dignity of every creature in the web of life. A profound humility, a gratitude for all of creation swept over me. In a kind of daze, I stumbled on ahead to find the bus to Gaza.

Minutes later I stepped down onto a steamy street amid a shouting, jostling throng of people. They pulled at my sleeves. Others pushed through, prodding their donkeys. Some of them begged, some stared vacantly. Hollow-eyed and painfully thin, jabbering children surrounded me. People were open and curious, even kindly, and although there was nothing threatening about the crowd, I was clearly out of place.

One young man spoke enough English to ask, "American?"

"Yes," I replied.

"American planes bombed here," he declared flatly.

Smiling, and momentarily at a loss for words, I started to deny it but caught myself, realizing that these people, with their millions and their military might, could not accept being defeated by the tiny country next door. As they saw it, Israel must have had help, and surely America had come to their aid! (In retrospect, who knows? Maybe there was really something to their belief.)

The scene before me shook me to the core. I had never witnessed such poverty and devastation. People lay hopelessly in the street, some barely moving, while others scurried around them on errands of survival.

I realized, again, that even though the citizens expressed curiosity and good will toward me, I stood out conspicuously among them. I knew I should leave while my luck held.

I was grateful for having glimpsed the world of Gaza, and the memory of these desperate, yet somehow hopeful, people would shape my understanding of this tumultuous region.

As the months passed on the little kibbutz, it became apparent to the residents that I wasn't just a casual, wayfaring visitor, and one day I was asked to drive the tractor. This was a step up from picking fruit, and an honor. While driving to the fields one morning, I heard for the first time the fulsome harmonies of the Mamas and the Papas singing "California

Dreamin'" on someone's transistor radio. It fired up pangs for the home I hadn't seen in almost four years.

"Settle man, settle!" a co-worker shouted as we crossed paths one evening after supper. The people of the settlement would have welcomed me if I chose to stay on and become an Israeli, sharing in their merry, chaotic, dangerous but hope-filled adventure. I was feeling so much at home and so comfortable in this open, friendly country that I was tempted to stay. Had I not been accepted to The American Musical & Dramatic Academy for the upcoming semester, I might well have taken them up on the offer. It was a bucolic setting, much to my liking, an alternative life wide open to the future.

As the month of April approached, it was time to say goodbye. I had been on Nir-Am for three months, and during that time, I had journeyed to the great sites of Jerusalem, the Dead Sea, Bethlehem, the Red Sea, Galilee, and Acre. Even as a volunteer, I had made friends among the people of the kibbutz, and for two or three years afterward, I received a yearly Christmas card from Nir-Am.

I made my way back, through Cyprus to Istanbul, then on the Orient Express to Frankfurt, Germany, to catch my flight back to the USA. I'd been away almost four years.

The country I came back to was no longer the place I'd left behind. Gone was the short- haired, gray conformity of the early sixties. When I stepped off the plane in New York in 1968, a long-haired, brightly spangled country pulsing with new life greeted me. A cultural revolution was sweeping the nation, and anything seemed possible. I couldn't wait to throw away my uniform, and eagerly set off for East 23rd Street to check in at The American Musical & Dramatic Academy.

My heart raced as I read over the daily curriculum for the next two years—acting, dance, speech, musical theatre, sight-singing, Shakespeare with Philip Burton, individual voice lessons. And thanks to a rat, and a ragtag family of adventurers on the Gaza Strip, a glow would illumine whatever lay ahead.

But first, I needed to pay a visit home. I boarded the Greyhound for the long, cross-country trip to San Mateo. As I walked up the familiar avenue, duffel bag over my shoulder, our old cat Skeeter, now approaching twenty, emerged from the shade under the trees and tottered unsteadily down the driveway to meet me. Four years had passed, but she remembered me, as she brushed against my leg and purred. It was a moment I would not forget.

I had just missed connecting with my sister Sue, whom I hadn't seen since I'd shipped out for Europe in the fall of 1964, nearly four years before. Just a few months earlier she had flown to Hawaii for a vacation. Falling under the spell of those islands, she had decided to stay on. As it turned out, she stayed on for seven years. We wouldn't see each other until 1975.

After a month at home, I returned to New York. There, on a bright spring day, I walked into a rehearsal room where fifteen other aspiring performers were gathered expectantly, and caught my first sight of a luminescent, sparkling-eyed young woman at the edge of the group.

But that's another story...

CHAPTER 8:
BEYOND ALPHABET CITY

It was 1968, one of the most tumultuous and consequential years in American history, and I was starting out at The American Musical and Dramatic Academy (AMDA). The year had begun with the Tet offensive in Vietnam, turning American public opinion against the war. It continued with the shock of Martin Luther King's assassination, and dozens of American cities exploding in fire and urban warfare. Two months later, Robert Kennedy, upon whom many of us had placed great hope, was gunned down on the verge of winning the Democratic nomination. While the country was going up in flames and Chicago police clashed in a blood bath with demonstrators at the Democratic Convention, Richard Nixon secured the Republican nomination. On the periphery of all this, we at AMDA continued in a kind of bubble, consumed by classes in acting, dance, speech, musical theatre, sight singing, Shakespeare, and individual voice lessons.

On the very first day at the Academy, my eyes had fallen on a lithe, dark-haired beauty of Irish descent named Anne. Her eyes twinkled with humor, and unlike some beautiful women I'd met, she seemed to be about far more than her physical allure. Her openness and quick mind, combined with a certain earthiness, made her irresistible.

Our "head shots," around the time we met, 1968.

Usually I brown-bagged it for lunch in an empty classroom at the school. But I managed to save a few dollars, and one day at our noon break, I found the words to ask Anne out to lunch. As we walked to the Middle Eastern restaurant up the street, I was startled and delighted by how easy and natural it was being with her.

The Leonard Cohen song "Suzanne" was popular in 1968. I had known a couple of Suzannes, girls of a certain mystique on the borderline of the world. Anne had that aura about her. One of the first things we spoke of that day, over hummus and babaganoush and stuffed grape leaves, was "Suzanne."

A few days later, I received a letter from *Poet Lore* magazine announcing that "Out of the West" had won Third Prize in the Stephen Vincent Benet Narrative Poetry Contest. Anne was the first person I shared the good news with.

The days and weeks followed in a euphoric haze as it dawned on me that Anne was "the one." As young as we were, our souls saw each other, and through all the wild years that followed, they would never forget.

At twenty-six I felt primed and ready, though I really wasn't. And neither was she.

Anne invited me home for dinner to meet her folks. Her dad, a renowned internist, arrived just before we sat down. The bond between the two of them was almost tangible as glances of love and deep knowing passed between them throughout dinner.

Seven days later Anne's father died of a heart attack. Our world crashed. Whatever was blooming between us was buried in grief and turmoil, and we suddenly found ourselves on separate paths.

As the day of the funeral approached, I knew I would not long have the chance to express what I was feeling, and I set about composing the most important letter of my life. It took me two days of all-out focus. As the hearse carrying the casket and the limo carrying Anne and the rest of her family pulled away to the cemetery, I looked into her eyes and slipped the letter into her hand through the open window.

With funds suddenly scarce after her father's demise, Anne's future at AMDA was in jeopardy. Recognizing her talents, Cliff Robertson and

Dina Merrill stepped in, awarding her a scholarship to complete the program over the next year.

After our class graduated in the spring of 1970, Anne departed for a series of lead roles in summer stock and touring companies, and we disappeared from each other's lives.

Though unfinished, it was ended, and Anne disappeared onto a back shelf of the mind. I had found the great love, and now it was not to be. A seal came down around my heart, and for many years after, relationships were short-lived.

Anne as Joan of Arc in *The Lark*.

Setting out stoically after graduation, I landed summer stock jobs in Massachusetts and Pennsylvania, and at Theatre by the Sea in Rhode Island. When I returned to Manhattan in the fall, I was hired to be an understudy in *Little Boxes*, an off-Broadway play by the British writer John Bowen.

But every night, I returned to the less illustrious world of my apartment, where I awoke one night to the sound of footsteps on the roof. Next the footsteps were heading down the hallway. I reached for the crowbar and listened intently at my door. When the steps were just out-side, I raised the crowbar over my head and whipped the door open.

"Please, Mr. Flanders! It's me, the landlord!" he bellowed in a German accent, eyes wide, hands up in surrender.

I stopped the swing in midair. Frozen, he displayed a row of gleam-ing teeth, reminding me of a wolf trying to smile

"Mr. Hindsmith, what are you doing?! It's the middle of the night!"

"I was just inspecting the roof," he muttered obsequiously, backing away. "I'm sorry to disturb you."

Paris, Israel, the army... none of it had prepared me for New York. Nothing could have. The apartment was in the depths of "alphabet city"—East 11th Street and Avenue C— and it was what I could afford. Cars burning in the street were a common sight, and gangs congregated in doorways, eyeing passersby. Prowlers had broken into an adjacent apartment, so when I heard footsteps on the roof, I thought the thieves were back.

The asphalt world of New York was soul deadening. In the bleakness of my surroundings, I summoned bucolic scenes from the movie *Friendly Persuasion* and lost myself in a book I'd spotted at an East Village book-store, *Pleasant Valley*. Meadows of clover, clear running springs, lowing cows, and a writer named Louis Bromfield, turning sod and reclaiming a farm in the Ohio sunshine, sustained me. Whenever I lost my way in those grey years and forgot what mattered, scenes from *Pleasant Valley* and its sequel, *Malabar Farm*, returned me to the land of the "great elm."

I leaped at any chance to escape my deadening surroundings, even for a short while. After performing *I Do, I Do* at a dinner theatre in Jackson, Mississippi, I returned to the apartment in New York. Larry, who had been the stage manager for *I Do, I Do*, was also the assistant to Bill Cullen, host of the popular game show, *Three on a Match*. Always sympathetic to struggling performers, Larry offered to get me on the show as a contestant to have a crack at some prize money. Even if I didn't win, I was assured a handsome consolation prize. It sounded promising, and I looked him up as soon as I returned to the city. In a well-worn sport coat and tie, I went down to the TV studio where Larry ushered me through a successful interview. His private instructions to me were firm – I couldn't let on that I knew him, and I could in no way reveal that I was an actor. When Bill Cullen briefly interviewed all three guest contestants live, on air, I would have to cite another profession. My assumption was that he would routinely ask our names and vocations, and rapidly move on with the show.

I didn't take much time deliberating, carelessly deciding to call myself a "writer," assuming that would fly by easily enough. Then the signal light flashed, and we three contestants were ushered onto the set to take our seats for the start of a new segment. Bill first addressed the girl next to me.

"I'm Kathy so-and-so, and I'm a mom."

"And George, what do you do?'

"Hi Bill," smiling smoothly, "I'm a plumber."

"And you're Rich Flanders, I see. What do you do, Rich?"

Attempting a mature smile, "I'm a writer."

"Oh? What do you write, Rich?"

I was dumbfounded. I had not thought beyond, "I'm a writer," expecting Bill would just move on as he always did. But today, for some reason, Bill was curious.

Shifting in my chair, turning red in the lengthening silence, I blurted out my brilliant response, "Oh, lots of things."

One eyebrow lifted on Bill's face as the audience waited expectantly. "Uh, right now I'm working on a couple of articles, and some poetry."

Bill stared a moment, then without missing a beat, he began his routine explanation of the rules of the show. Flushed with embarrassment, I stumbled through the rest of the show, winding up in last place and doing my best to be invisible. As I slunk off the set, a red-faced Larry said nothing and was barely able to contain his own mortification. Walking home, I dearly hoped that nobody I knew had seen the debacle. At least I'd be receiving a generous thank you gift, as promised, for being on the show.

One evening a few weeks later, I arrived at the apartment to find four enormous boxes at my door marked, *Three on a Match*. I looked hard but found no accompanying envelope with a check. Dubiously, I began to open the boxes. The scent that wafted from them should have alerted me. I flipped back the cardboard to reveal stacks of Camay soap bars. I'd at least be a clean, out of work actor.

Corinna, a girl who had been an apprentice at one of the summer theatres, invited me to Sunday dinner at the family home in Long Island. I had no inkling of what Sunday dinner with her Italian family might entail. Not always certain where my next meal would come from, I dove into the first course and the second course and was into the third course before I realized there were several more to come, and just as hearty. All the relatives, dressed in their Sunday best, were solicitous that I get enough to eat, and I was full before the meal was halfway served.

From her end of the long dining table, Corinna called to her mother at the other end: "Mom, I just don't want the job at Bergdorf's."

"Well, do you want a job at the airport?"

"Naw, I don't want to work at the airport."

"How about working with Uncle Sal?"

"Well, I dunno."

And so it went, and as I watched this familial exchange, something inside me took note. The conversation turned to the problem of crime in the streets. The fellow across from me, clean-cut in sportscoat and tie, in his forties, railed against it. Living in "alphabet city," I opined that crime in the streets was something I was seeing plenty of, firsthand.

"I know, I know," my new friend sympathized. "It's terrible."

Then, leaning in and looking me in the eye, he asked quietly, "Rich, you wanna' gun?"

I stared for just a moment, then, stammered. "Well, I don't know."

Actually, it sounded like a great idea.

Fortunately, I'd just seen *The Godfather*, and was dimly beginning to piece together the meaning of the conversation between Corinna and her mother, and the offer of a gun. I was having a pleasant Sunday dinner . . . with a crime family.

"Well, what about serial numbers?" I stalled.

"Don't worry about it."

Laughing nervously, "Well, let me think it over. And thanks." And with that, the conversation drifted elsewhere, and I made my escape from what could have been a tricky future.

Not long after that Philip Burton, who had taught us at AMDA and who was Richard Burton's mentor and namesake, cast me with three other AMDA graduates in a show he'd created that traced the history of the American Musical. Directed by fellow AMDA alumni Victoria Mallory, fresh from starring in the Lincoln Center revival of *West Side Story,* the show toured colleges across the country.

When the tour ended months later, I returned again to New York and took a job as a singing waiter at a posh East Side steakhouse, but soon afterwards, my tolerance for life in alphabet city finally reached its limits. With great relief, I quit Manhattan and embarked on years of playing dinner theatre, regional theatre, and summer stock across the country. I was glad to give up the apartment, escape the sordidness of alphabet city, and play challenging roles to appreciative audiences across the nation. Through the rootless years of the early seventies performing out of a suitcase, I would find an anchor not only in the pages of *Pleasant Valley,* but most memorably in four golden summers at Rhode Island's Theatre by the Sea. There I not only found artistic fulfillment in such plays as *Promises, Promises* and *1776,* but I found nourishment for the soul amid the fields, woods, and crashing surf of the idyllic summer theatre. Days under the great elm returned, cleansing my spirit and reminding me of what mattered.

CHAPTER 9:
BROADWAY BIWAYS

After several years of bouncing from town to town and theatre to theatre, I decided to accept an offer from an actor friend to take up residence in the back room of his apartment on the lower East Side. At the moment, my prospects looked grim. I had twelve dollars in my wallet. My unemployment insurance had just run out, and I had no idea what would open up when my last dollar was gone. I was curiously unconcerned about that, but on this fall evening in September of 1975, I was about to find out.

A buddy dropped in and mentioned that the producer of the Broadway hit *Shenandoah* was holding auditions in his office for the show's first replacement.

"What, now? Tonight?!"

After a stunned moment, I sprang into audition clothes, ran to the subway, raced down the street to the office building, sped up the stairs to the producer's office and breathlessly took a seat in the anteroom, where I waited for my turn. I had kept the voice in shape, vocalizing daily, no matter what conditions I was living in. That was now about to pay off. Knowing the show's score had a Rodgers and Hammerstein feel, I chose "Soliloquy" from *Carousel* for my audition piece.

The next day my friends and I celebrated when the call came telling me that I was hired. I would set about learning the several small roles assigned to me, as well as understudy "Sam," one of the leads.

I had reached one of the pinnacles of success in the profession—performing on Broadway. A critical and commercial hit, as well as a memorable anti-war statement, *Shenandoah* transformed the life of a wayfaring actor. In an instant my fortunes had catapulted from twelve dollars and no future, to several hundred dollars a week for the foreseeable future. I would embrace a new standard of living and find an apartment of my own. I would stay with the show for two years, until it closed in the fall of 1977—but not before the play, and my newfound success, nearly met an untimely end.

I had only been in the show a few weeks when the musicians suddenly went on strike. *Shenandoah*, and all of Broadway, closed down. I had just been handed the biggest break of my life, and now it was going to be taken back? My parents had already booked a flight east to see their son on Broadway and celebrate with me. My sister Sue, who had just returned to California from eight years in Hawaii, was now gallantly driving across the country with her five-year-old daughter, Kris, in a barely functioning car, to join us in New York. We hadn't seen each other in eleven years. I'd looked forward to reuniting with her under brighter circumstances and meeting my new niece, whose name was like a song—Kristan Kiele Navia. "Kristan" and "Navia" honored her Scandinavian and Philippine-Polynesian heritage, and "Kiele," the Polynesian word for "gardenia," evoked the scent of the trade winds of Hawaii.

My sense of unfairness was mounting.

Actors and stagehands were suddenly without work, and parking garages, restaurants, taxi drivers, and theatre owners were in a tailspin. I huddled with Ted, one of the principals, who was just as determined as I to get the Broadway shows open again. With every precious passing day, our desperation grew. We couldn't be union busters, but how could we pressure the two sides to end the impasse and save the shows? Our minds spun furiously "out of the box," and finally hatched a novel idea. With all the shows shut down, Shubert Alley, in the center of the theatre district, was empty. Why not put on mini versions of all the closed shows in Shubert Alley at noon time! We spread the word, and the casts up and down Broadway loved the idea. On a busy Friday at lunchtime, surprised tourists and office workers thronged in delight to see the stars and hear a cappella excerpts from Broadway shows for free. New York loved it, and hope stayed alive.

Still, the strike dragged on. Brainstorming, Ted and I recalled the protests of the 1960s, and suddenly our faces lit up. We'll march! We would create a star-studded spectacle, and just like the performances in Shubert Alley, the march would get publicity in all the papers. Once again, the casts of the shows loved the idea, and on the very next Sunday afternoon, hundreds of performers met on the West Side. With *Shenandoah* proudly leading off, the casts of *Grease, The Magic Show, Same Time, Next Year, Chicago, Pippin,* and a couple dozen other Broadway shows, with stars like Ellen Burstyn, John Cullum, Gwen Verdun, Betty Buckley, and Alan Alda, stepped off from 42nd Street, banners flying. We marched, sang, laughed, and danced our way past cheering crowds and dark theatres straight up Broadway to 57th Street. Howard Cosell and other newscasters followed alongside the marchers, interviewing and commentating.

At one point I spotted some reporters with notepads and pencils in hand just ahead. Assuming an air of leadership, I made eye contact with one of them. He ran up alongside me and began asking questions, as if I were the one in charge. I did nothing to dissuade him from that impression.

"How long will this strike last?"

"I have no idea."

"How much is this costing the city?"

Without hesitation, "About a million dollars a day."

"Thank you, very much," he said, madly scribbling, and scurried off.

Nothing could have surprised or delighted us more than seeing the front-page article in *The New York Times* the next day:

Strike costing city a million dollars a day, sources say . . .

The next week, *TIME* magazine reposted the reporting from the *Times*, and the sobering figure of a million dollars a day became accepted as reality. It may have been a million, it may have been much more, but "a million dollars a day" was the new catch phrase, and it dominated the negotiating table. A few creative moments with a fledgling *New York Times* reporter resulted in a speedier end to the strike than any other action we could have taken.

I learned something about the news business that day. And my credo to always "take chances" had been proven out once again.

Several of the plays, such as *The Magic Show*, couldn't outlast the strike and folded. But *Shenandoah* somehow held on, and the night we reopened was unforgettable. As the overture played and the curtain rose on our Civil War tableau, a cheering audience surged to its feet, and the applause swelled. Our show, beloved by so many, had survived.

During these years I kept up weekly voice lessons as steadily as I could, trekking over to the studio of Paul Gavert near Carnegie Hall. Until enrolling at the American Musical & Dramatic Academy in 1968, acting was my forte. I'd had no prior training in voice. Green and fresh, I was lucky to have been assigned to Paul for voice training at AMDA. His career had been launched in a 1945 London production of *Song of Norway*, and he subsequently earned renown as an international performer of German "lieder," and for a memorable concert at Town Hall in Manhattan. Now, as a voice teacher, he aimed to uncover the voice within. He saw something in me, nurturing it until he died in 1992. There were occasions when I had no money to pay him, but Paul wouldn't hear of my missing a session. He became almost like a father, and his faith in me was a constant inspiration.

The Paul Gavert studio was legendary, and entertainment royalty passed in and out of its doors. I would often exchange a nod with Joel Grey, and other students included Sting, Jose Ferrer, Len Cariou, Jane Seymour, Ron Perlman, and Treat Williams. Two of Paul's young protégés, Vicky Mallory and Kurt Peterson, who graduated ahead of me at AMDA, had now become Broadway stars. The studio was like a second home to them. Mark Planner in the cast of *Godspell* would later become one of Paul's protégés, and when I returned to the studio decades later to take up voice again, Mark would be my teacher.

Betty Buckley, one of Paul's most noted students, had her lesson before mine. From within the studio, I could hear the thrilling rendition of "Memories" she was preparing for *Cats*. Paul's reputation for helping to develop, and sometimes save, the voices of the cast members of *A Chorus Line, Chicago, A Little Night Music* and other shows became so well known that Stephen Sondheim asked to have a lesson with Paul, just to see what the magic was all about.

Paul showed us how to "follow" the voice, not struggle to produce it. A fierce, kind love shone from his eyes, and he drew out the same powerful force in his students. No one who knew him was not the better for it.

In the spring of 1977, luck smiled again. As I hurried past the line in front of the theatre, heading for the stage door, someone shouted, "Hey, Rich!" I paused to see who it was and met the eyes of a girl I'd known at the Academy, Kathy, standing in line to see *Shenandoah*. We agreed to meet after the show.

Seated across from me in the coffeeshop, Kathy asked if I'd ever heard of "Shaklee." I grew intrigued as she told me the story of the visionary Dr. Forrest Shaklee, creator of the world's first multivitamin back in 1915, a product he called "Vitalized Minerals." He was a man who "listened to nature, then did what she told me." The supplements were not vitamins per se, but pure, balanced foods of the highest quality. If I tried them and didn't feel better, no matter how well I may have been feeling initially, I could get all my money back. If the products were that good, I thought, then there must be something to the income opportunity. I was aware of the poor nutritional content of American food, and my physical health was like an avocation for me.

It took only three days on the "basic program" for me to begin to note physical changes. I was waking up feeling more refreshed, and on less sleep. I no longer needed coffee in the morning to clear away the cobwebs. My energy was increasing, as well as my physical endurance. As the weeks passed, my ability to focus improved, and my skin looked healthier. It was clear that something extraordinary was happening. This was real. No matter how discerning I thought I'd been in my food choices, my body evidently had not been getting complete, high-quality nutrition. The physical changes continued, driving me to tell others about Shaklee. I was about to embark on a life-changing adventure.

I said to my best friend, Marshall, sitting a couple chairs up from me in the dressing room, "You're getting this!" Within a week, he too began to feel better. Friends and family who experienced the supplements were excited about the changes in their health, and I soon found myself with a fledgling organization. It was as if a light had broken through the grey world of show business. The farm boy within was excited by a company rooted in nature, a company that was a force for pure good in the world. The company was structured so that you could only prosper to the degree that you succeeded in helping others. That was a principal I could get behind. By the time *Shenandoah* closed in the fall of 1977, I was set on building an enterprise that would liberate me from having to work for others, while doing something I believed in.

Shortly after the show closed, I had a vivid dream that I was cast in the new mega hit, *Annie*. So, when I went to audition for the first national tour of the show, I knew I already had the job. Relaxed and confident, I sailed through the audition and was hired immediately.

The team who'd captained the Broadway production was now in charge of ours, the first national touring company. Early on in our rehearsals the contrast between creative acting and cartoon performance came into sharp relief. In my role as "swing," understudying five of the lesser roles, I began to grow bored with direction that seemed aimed at robotic performance. It was an approach that by its very nature couldn't tap the full creative juices of an actor. I quipped to a pal that the dog had the best part. At the same time, my interest in creating healthier lives, working with real people, was growing.

Supercilious and sometimes even disdainful towards the actors, those in charge seemed strangely removed from the reality of actors' lives and the gritty world beyond the stage. From the back of the theatre the bark of the director would correct a performer, all too often accompanied by personal insult and the fawning chuckles of subordinates.

Michael, a short, unprepossessing performer, was the butt of many of the demeaning remarks. "Can't you move faster?" "You might want to spend less time kibbitzing and more time learning your lines." "We can't hear you. Don't you know about projection?" No matter how belittling the comments, Michael smiled tightly, took the correction, and quietly continued.

Ever drawn to underdogs, I began to take an interest in Michael. In the calm of the dressing room, he ate slowly for a few minutes in silence. Then he looked at me, eyes blazing, and let loose. "That chicken shit son of a bitch! These candy asses aren't worth spit!"

I listened and learned. Quiet, diligent, nondescript Michael, now making a modest living as a supporting performer, had once waded through the bloody surf of Saipan, his fellow Marines going down all around him in one of the most horrific landings of World War 2. He had received wounds that would forever impede his ability to digest food, and had seen things no Broadway actor, producer, or director was ever likely to see. Yet here he was, invisible amidst the effete purveyors of a cartoon-style New York musical.

The most fun I had in *Annie* was wandering into Gary Beach's dressing room and immediately falling into wild improvisations. I usually had trouble getting through them without breaking up. Gary was one of the most talented, versatile performers I'd ever known, and I always snuck out front to watch the famous *Easy Street* number whenever I could. Later on, he was a standout playing Hitler in the play and film version of *The Producers*.

I couldn't help but notice that I was having more fun talking about Shaklee on the phone than playing mechanical roles, and after eight months performing *Annie* in Toronto, Miami, St. Louis, and Washington, DC, I gave my notice and returned to New York. I rented a one-bedroom apartment on 70th and Broadway and dove headlong into the Shaklee business with excited friends. For those of us in the jaded world of show business, the wholesomeness of Shaklee was irresistible. With joy and ease, we built thriving Shaklee groups from the little apartment on the upper West Side.

This was also a time of exploration dubbed "The New Age." Health food stores sprang up everywhere, along with a plethora of weekend workshops on "Mind Control," "The Power of Acknowledgement," "EST," and its spin-off, "Actualizations." During a closed-eye process at the graduation ceremony of "Actualizations," a vision spread before me of a white draped dais, glittering with jewels.

It symbolized my life—past, present, and future.

During a weekend on "The Power of Acknowledgment," I was seated across from a partner engaged in an exercise that required us to lock eyes. You couldn't look away under any circumstances. Soon, as time fell away, I lost touch with the surroundings. In that vacuum a soft, easy laughter began to bubble up from some place deep within, soundlessly at first. Never taking my eyes from my partner's eyes, the laughter became audible as a tingling, pleasing sensation rippled up my spine and through the top of my head. As it did so I seemed at one with my soul, floating in the universe. It was as if I were experiencing my essence bubbling up and through me like a fountain. What was that essence? An impersonal ecstatic Joy!

Just below our emotions and our thoughts, which seem so tangible, lies who we are—filaments of an evanescent Joy streaming from the heart of the universe. We are all, by nature, "enlightened."

I had glimpsed something eternal. I was not meant to forget it.

Since the move from Illinois to California, I had thrown up a shield around a heart that I'd discovered was too soft. When Anne and I met at AMDA the shield dissolved. But after we parted, the shield snapped back into place. It would encumber romantic encounters for many years.

Decades of movies inevitably morphed into my psyche and colored my understanding of how to be in the world. But I was not Glenn Ford or

William Holden, the women were not Elizabeth Taylor or Kim Novak, and the movie wasn't *Friendly Persuasion*, though I strove for it to be.

After a final out-of-sync disaster with an impossibly perfect blonde—beautiful, talented, and funny, but not for me—I dropped the trappings of romance in disgust and fell, exhausted, back into my heart. That was where I belonged, and landing there felt warm and right, even if it meant being alone. After all, I was really just the kid who loved roaming in the wild iris, protecting the family of rabbits in the garden, and singing in harmony. I was not leathery Randolph Scott or implacable John Wayne or even easy-going Joel McCrea, my favorite. They had served me well in life as role models of honesty, integrity, and courage. But I was done trying to hide who I was. For better or worse, I was just myself now, take it or leave it.

Almost immediately, the universe responded.

In the spring of 1981, I held a convention at the Holiday Inn on Manhattan's lower West Side for my growing Shaklee organization. I turned around in my chair and found myself looking into the eyes of a girl who could have been straight out of the sixties. With her clear, steady, no-nonsense gaze, beaded necklace, granny dress, and cascading chestnut hair she resembled a flower child. This was Amy, and we would be together for thirty-one years.

But that's another story . . .

CHAPTER 10:
POSSUMS – AND OTHER MASTERS

Just in time I swerved to miss the animal lying still in the road, apparently dead. But as our car drew alongside the animal, one of its legs began to slowly stretch upwards.

"STOP!" cried Amy, but I had already caught the movement, and swung the car violently around to the side of the road.

We sprang out, waving traffic on, and ran to him. His jaw was bloody and hung a little unevenly, but other than that, we saw no visible injuries on what looked like a possum. Momentarily at a loss to know what to do, I instinctively reached forward and touched its tail. Instantly the tail wrapped around my finger, and we realized that this was how we could get him off the road. Hanging from my finger, I gently laid him in the grass. Amy ran to the inn that was just up the road.

Minutes later, she came back with rags and a cardboard box to put him in. We couldn't leave him there on the roadside. We had no choice but to take him with us to the "no animals allowed" motel where we would spend the night. We would try to find a vet in the morning. We had driven up the coast to visit Theatre by the Sea, so I could share a cherished part of my earlier life with Amy, only to find ourselves in an encounter that would be pivotal to our relationship.

The meow-like cries of the possum through the night were heartbreaking. We were helpless to do more than give him water and a soft bed. But at dawn the next morning we ran out to the phone booth and scrambled through the yellow pages for a vet clinic that might be open on Labor Day in Rhode Island. We dialed and dialed with no luck until we got to the last vet on the list. A young apprentice who had drawn holiday duty told us to bring in the possum as soon as we could. Rushing back up the stairs to our room we heard a shriek, and then saw the maid hurrying out of our room, ashen faced. We had neglected to alert her about the wild creature in the cardboard box.

The teenage girl at the vet clinic was a critter whisperer. She smiled and took over, gently but firmly lifting our friend out of the box and onto the table. Her quick exam revealed that the possum had a broken jaw and was missing a couple of teeth, but she said that he should recover. In our beaming smiles, Amy and I saw in each other the same inclination to protect the helpless and the vulnerable, and the same crazy adoration for creatures. As Amy later told friends, "My father would have kept driving." We couldn't quite have put it into words, but we knew that something had been deeply stirred within both of us.

We had a bottle of one of Shaklee's tonics with us, loaded with nutrients, that we left with the vet tech on the promise that she would include it in his daily feeding. Wistful, but deeply content, we drove away, vowing to check in regularly.

In the weeks that followed, we were delighted to hear that he was steadily healing. About two months later, we called and heard that our boy, now fully recovered, had padded to the back door of the clinic, refusing to budge. His caretakers sensed that the little fellow knew best, and that it was time for him to return to the forest. They opened the door and watched him walk straight to the woods, never looking back. We knew we had done the right thing. Others may find the face of a possum off-putting. But for us from then on, no creature was cuter.

In the spring of 1983, Amy and I were invited to a yoga center in Manhattan to hear a pair of speakers that a friend had spoken highly of. But the speakers were late, and we hadn't yet had dinner. Growing hungry, and tired of sipping exotic teas, we decided to leave. We'd had it with yet another flaky "New Age" event. Donning our coats, we walked briskly to the exit to go find a restaurant. As we neared the revolving doors, I looked into the eyes of a tall, white-mustached man and his striking female companion as they approached. Something stirred inside. I tugged Amy's arm, "I'm staying." But she, too, had seen them. Without a word, we put the idea of dinner aside and followed the speakers back inside.

These were the Lindwalls, "Doc" and Ruth, who had pioneered a soul-shaking new healing modality called "Releasing." Three years later they would marry us, and for the next twenty-five years they would be teachers, mentors, and traveling companions—but most of all, they would be cherished family.

"Doc," a chiropractic physician by trade, had one driving passion— to find the primary cause of pain and help alleviate suffering. In a lifelong search he had seen, time and again, how symptoms often returned even after expert medical treatments. Devoted to "Spirit," or "Source," as he termed it, Doc had sought guidance in study and meditation for years.

One day while in a session with a patient, he began to receive puzzling phrases in his mind, and a knowing that the patient should repeat them aloud: "Release hatred of your brother in Egypt," "Release envy of your mother in Galicia," "Release your rage at so-and-so in France."

To Doc's amazement, when the patient repeated the channeled phrases aloud, the pain was neutralized, and spinal manipulation was unnecessary. Was this process actually deprogramming the cells' memories, and had those cellular memories originated in a patient's past life?

Understanding time in the context of "past lives" may have been a concept beyond the mind's ability to grasp, but the idea of releasing past life memories in present time served as a working construct. As further experiences with patients unfolded, it became evident that there were three different forms of negative cellular memories. In addition to past life memories, there were of course the memories recorded on cells within the current lifetime. Additionally, it seemed that cells could hold what appeared to be genetic memories. Negative memories held in the cells of the body, whether originating from past life, current life, or genetic inheritance, created limiting life patterns. The process of releasing them could neutralize their negativity. The words "I release..." spoken aloud, seemed to discharge the stored energy—much like hitting the delete command on the computer. The ultimate goal of the Releasing process was Neutrality. In a space of neutrality an individual had the freedom and clarity to make more conscious choices.

As Doc continued on his path, which struck a chord in us for its selflessness and purity, he began to see clairvoyantly. Time after time, Amy and I witnessed this phenomenon. At a restaurant, he might look at a cashier or a cook or a waiter and "see" that his or her liver was out of balance, or their shoulder or left foot needed realignment.

"Would you like me to help you with your right arm?" he asked on one occasion.

The startled waiter was momentarily speechless. How could this stranger have "seen" that his right arm habitually ached? Looking into the kind, clear blue eyes and Santa Claus face of Doc Lindwall, he relaxed and said, "Sure!" not knowing what to expect.

Doc closed his eyes to receive an inner direction. Then he asked the waiter to repeat aloud the phrase he'd heard: "I release..." Sometimes, as in this case, the process only took a few moments. Broadly smiling, the waiter wrapped Doc in a bear hug, after which we went on with our dinner. Whenever Doc Lindwall saw suffering that he might be able to alleviate, he answered the call, no matter where.

The releasing work was not magic, though it might appear as such to many. Although Doc's work was based on esoteric or "metaphysical" principles, it was clearly grounded in scientific principles as well. Being a chiropractor by trade, Doc was rigorous in applying scientific foundations to this work. Certified in Kinesiology, he was able to establish the link between the muscle groups associated with various organs and the corresponding negative emotions, such as hate, fear, jealousy, envy, etc. These connections were verified through kinesiological "testing" of muscle groups.

For example, grief affects the lungs; over-responsibility affects the shoulders and upper back; hate, the thymus; self-disgust, the stomach; fear and distrust, the spleen, etc. Identifying a particular trapped emotion, such as over-responsibility for someone in a past life, and then releasing it verbally, frees poisonous trapped energy. Amy and I personally experienced this healing phenomenon and witnessed it happen for others on countless occasions.

Word of the effectiveness of the Releasing work spread throughout the United States, and the Lindwalls began to teach the theory and practice in workshops. They called it "Freedom Through Releasing." Soon they were traveling beyond the United States to Germany, Italy,

France, Canada, South Africa, and later to the Iron Curtain countries of
Rumania and Hungary.

"Doc" and Ruth

Diving headlong into the "releasing" process, Amy and I encountered our own deeply rooted patterns. As we worked the process, experiencing the liberating, healing qualities of the Releasing technique,
we gradually became facilitators ourselves. Soon we began assisting the
Lindwalls with workshops in New York, and traveled with them to cities
like Austin, Atlanta, and Halifax, Nova Scotia. As the years passed, we
became certified releasing practitioners, working with other practitioners
alongside the Lindwalls in weekend events that were becoming increas-
ingly large.

Releasing "limiting patterns" would become an ongoing, lifelong
practice, as Amy and I discovered. Our souls were drawing together, but
at the personality level we often clashed. I was from Norman Rockwell
America; Amy, from a secular New York Jewish background. Our
conflicts were sometimes fierce, but almost always ended with some
humorous quip. The possum had sealed our hearts, but our intermittent

disharmony was enough to hold the idea of marriage at arm's length. The releasing practice, along with other healing disciplines, helped to neutralize the discord between us, until "our five-year whirlwind courtship," as Amy sardonically quipped, finally came to an end.

We were married by the Lindwalls in 1986 at the historic old Connecticut home of one of our Shaklee members. We had written our own vows, and the lyrical, pastoral ceremony incorporated Shakespeare and the title song from our favorite movie, *Friendly Persuasion*. During dinner on the lawn afterwards, my dad sat in briefly on drums, and then surprised us all when he rose to sing, "I Only Have Eyes for You," moving my mother to shed a tear. This was their special song; one he had sung to her many times over the years.

Amy and I were both of the earth, at one with animals and all living things. From our life experiences, we knew we were different from others.

"You two are such tender grapes," Ruth observed.

Now no longer adrift, we shared a heart.

We found a sturdy pre-Civil War farmhouse with wide-plank oak floors and shady, ancient maples on Van Auken Creek outside the village of Waymart, near Honesdale, Pennsylvania, a town that would have special significance years later. The place brought back the bucolic life I had missed since my boyhood in Illinois. Eagerly, I turned over the rich river-bottom soil to create our first "organic" garden. The soft-eyed deer came, peering curiously through the living room window. And almost every day we delighted in visits from our neighbors—raccoons, rabbits, a snapping turtle, a Great Blue Heron. Soon Amy, though born and bred in Manhattan, became enamored of the rural life. With the help of Ruth, who'd been an interior designer, she fashioned a simple, warm country home. It would be our haven through the growth and exploration of the coming years.

Country pleasures, first home, Waymart, Pennsylvania, fall 1986.

CHAPTER 11:
THE GURU'S GIFTS

As seductive as our surroundings were, we missed the richness of life beyond the woods. Creating a home, tending a teeming garden, traveling through Pennsylvania and New York to build Shaklee businesses, and accompanying the Lindwalls in their workshops around the country were not enough. Amy had a calling, a gift for listening and seeing, and a healing presence with people. It was a gift that would not be denied. She set her sights on becoming a psychotherapist. Once a week we would drive two and a half hours to our West Side apartment so that she could earn a master's degree in Clinical Social Work at New York University. While in the city, I took the opportunity to continue vocal coaching with Paul Gavert. A long way from my former New York life in the theater, and busily involved in the leadership of my Shaklee organization, I needed to remind myself that I was primarily still a performer.

In 1988 we heard of a spiritual master in India named Sri Satya Sai Baba. Our souls lit up, eager to experience the mystical treasures of the East, and that summer we flew to India with the Lindwalls and a group of twenty of their German students. Landing in Bangalore, we made our way through a sea of scarlet, yellow, green, purple, and orange saris, plodding elephants, water buffalo, and leaping monkeys to a road lined with battered-looking taxis. Then it was a bumpy three-hour ride through red clay hills, with two muddy tea stops, to Sai Baba's ashram outside the village of Puttaparti, situated in tropical southern India.

A tall obelisk with the symbols of all the world's religions stood at the entrance of the ashram. Sai Baba's symbol of Divine Love at the top of the obelisk unified them all and welcomed everyone. Pilgrims of all faiths and backgrounds, as well as those who were just curious, had journeyed there from distant points in India and from countries all over the world. Several thousand people were housed on the grounds of the ashram, and we set up our sleeping bags and mosquito netting in a football-stadium-sized, cement-floored auditorium with families from South America, Europe, Malaysia, Australia, Canada, and the United States.

Soon after arriving, we heard the tale of a strapping young Australian athlete who'd walked in fresh and healthy one morning, ventured outside the ashram to eat lunch in Puttaparti, came back dizzy and vomiting, and in the space of a few hours, wasted away before their eyes. He lapsed into unconsciousness and died before dinner. The water and food on the ashram were safe. You took your chances on the outside.

The entrance to the ashram of Sri Satya Sai Baba, 1988.

Being seen by Sai Baba or seeing him anywhere on the ashram grounds was called a "darshan." It was considered a holy event of great good fortune. So each morning thousands of pilgrims gathered silently in front of the temple awaiting Sai Baba's emergence, hoping to be "seen" by him. At some point after he had walked out of the temple, he would beckon to someone in the throng and they would follow him back inside for a personal encounter. Many tales are told of the experiences of enlightenment, even of miracles, that unfolded at these times. Being chosen for a private darshan with Sai Baba was devoutly sought.

During our two weeks on the ashram, we found ourselves in close friendship with many of the Germans, who seemed familiar—like long-lost brothers and sisters, even though we had only recently been thrown together. Now many of them were growing impatient, frustrated that Sai Baba had not yet "seen" them or summoned them for a private interview.

They took to wearing uniform red scarves in hopes of attracting his attention as he passed through the throngs each morning. When that produced no results, they held a meeting and came up with a plan. When Sai Baba passed by the next morning, one of them would give a signal, and they would shout his name in unison so loud that he couldn't fail to take notice.

They encouraged Amy and me, Doc and Ruth, and the two or three other Americans and Canadians in the group to join them on this plan. We thanked them but graciously declined. We needed to listen to our own inner guidance.

The next morning as Sai Baba slowly passed by, looking straight ahead, the Germans on cue gave out a resounding shout. Almost imperceptibly, he turned his head in their direction and said quietly, "Germans, watch out!"

Our German sisters and brothers never got an interview, but they perhaps understood Sai Baba's gentle, historical reminder not to gang together to force an outcome. Not bad guidance in general.

Amy, on the other hand, had her own very special darshan. One afternoon, while seated alone on a boulder at the far reaches of the ashram, with her eyes closed in a reverie, Sai Baba came walking slowly down the path, passing only a few feet away from her. She never saw him, except in her mind's eye, but was later told of what had transpired by an observer. Unsought after, while in an inward state of harmony and love, she had experienced the perfect "darshan."

Everyone moved at a slow pace, and we steadily lost weight in that tropical air. There was a heightened energy of another kind on the ashram. It was a place of little miracles, or "leelas," whereby one's inner scenarios took on a life of their own and played out before your eyes. In a meditative state early one morning, I felt a longing for a dog. Immediately, a picture of a russet and white spaniel appeared in my mind's eye, reminiscent of Robert Mitchum's striking hunting dogs in *Home from the Hill.*

Before flying home, we traveled from the ashram with Doc and Ruth to Glastonbury, England, a place of special significance to Amy, who had performed in the ancient "miracle plays" there in the ruins of the great Abbey during her summers between semesters at Barnard college. Because it held a central place in the Arthurian legends, Glastonbury was a cauldron of diverse spiritual traditions from around the world, and we found ourselves amid a whirlwind of "releases" connected to those events.

Later that year, back home in Pennsylvania, we relished a great new novel based on the Arthurian legend written from the feminine perspective, *The Mists of Avalon.* Inspired by the characters in those pages, Amy began to refer to some men as "sons of the Goddess," men who carried the "divine feminine" energy.

We had been back for about two months and were enjoying an autumn Sunday breakfast in our Pennsylvania farmhouse when there was a knock on the door. It was a passing motorist, who asked us, "Is that your dog in the road?"

"What dog?"

We followed him up the lane to the highway, Route 6, where an injured dog lay on its side, locking eyes with us. He was almost a spitting image of the dog that had appeared to me in my vision in India.

He was severely hurt, but we carefully lifted him into our car and drove to the vet up the road. All the way there he lay silently against Amy's breast, never breaking his gaze into her eyes. I was determined that what had happened to "Tippy," the cat left to fend for herself and her kittens as we drove away from Western Springs all those years ago, was not about to happen to this fellow.

We asked where he had come from and what his story was, but all we ever found out was that he'd been abandoned. "He was thrown out of a car on Route 6," a passing motorist had told the vet. Then he'd been hit by a car and abandoned again.

Because of his red coloring, and because we liked the snob appeal of the more poetic Irish word for red, we called him "Rory." And so began many years of inseparable companionship.

From the beginning it was always the three of us—Amy, Rich, and Rory. Whenever we embarked on a journey in the car, he made sure he was lifted into the back seat, his home on the road, where he could keep an eye on us. He would recover from most of his injuries but would be lame in his right hind leg, slowing him down and inhibiting his ability to jump. We called him our angel dog because of his sweet, even, caring temperament.

Soul Mates   Brothers

Amy, Rory, Doc and Ruth...Family.

Since boyhood, I had suffered from severe allergies to spring pollen and fall ragweed. Amy and I had returned from India in the midst of the allergy season in fall 1988, yet I noted to my astonishment that I wasn't suffering from any symptoms. For the first time in my life, I was not choking, coughing, wheezing, and nearly ready for a trip to the emergency room. I have been free from fall allergies ever since. I've always considered it a gift from Sai Baba, making it easier for me to bring my singing voice into the world.

But Rory was Sai Baba's greatest gift, a four-legged guardian angel, always by our side to keep our hearts open.

CHAPTER 12:
THE KALALAU TRAIL

The loveliest fleet of islands that lies anchored in any ocean... No alien land in all the world has any deep strong charm for me but that one, no other land could so longingly and so beseechingly haunt me, sleeping and waking, through half a lifetime, as that one has done. Other things leave me, but it abides; other things change, but it remains the same.

For me the balmy airs are always blowing, its summer seas flashing in the sun; the pulsing of its surf beat is in my ear; I can see its garlanded crags, its leaping cascades, its plumy palms drowsing by the shore, its remote summits floating like islands above the cloud wrack; I can feel the spirit of its wildland solitudes, I can hear the splash of its brooks; in my nostrils still lives the breath of flowers that perished twenty years ago. –Mark Twain

At our house on Van Auken Creek, and later, when living in the old colonial in the Hudson Valley, Amy and I would pack our bags every summer for the luxury trip for qualified Shaklee leaders. The trips were the highlight of our year, excursions to magical destinations we never could have afforded to visit—Vienna, Madrid, Acapulco, Monte Carlo, London, Lucerne, cruising the Caribbean, sailing up the St. Lawrence waterway to Montreal. But for us, Hawaii eclipsed them all, and in eight trips there through the years, we explored every one of its islands but Niihau and Lanai. Whether the official Shaklee destination was Oahu, Maui, or the Big Island, we always set aside precious extra weeks for "the heart chakra of the planet," Kauai.

Here on this island, the inspiration for the ballad, "Bali Hai" in *South Pacific*, body and soul are caressed by the elements.

Trade winds carrying the scent of ginger and orchids awakened us at the first streaks of dawn on our first morning in Kauai. Because of the time difference, we were fully rested. We walked across the sand and slid into a clear, warm sea. Stroking leisurely as I swam on my back through the sparkling water, I smiled up at an impossibly blue sky, a song about to burst from my heart. We glided through the blue-green sea alongside schools of curious multicolored fish, and the occasional eel or small sand shark. To Amy's delight, an enormous sea turtle suddenly appeared over my shoulder, and dolphins sported not far away. Down the shore the elephant seal, returning from her yearly pilgrimage to her birthplace, clambered up to sun herself on a flat rock. We emerged dripping from the surf like a couple of sea creatures, and walked into the mango grove flanking the beach, where we picked up fresh fallen fruit for breakfast.

After a day in the sea and sun, we showered and dressed. I donned a flowered shirt and Amy chose an equally bright kimono, and we drove through the sunset to Tahiti Nui's. Just ahead, all but hidden in the thick palms, we spotted flickering torches and a bamboo and palm-frond shack straight out of Jack London. Ranged at the bar were the regulars—sun-blackened, t-shirted local boatmen and fishermen. At a wooden, candlelit table we dined on fresh mahi-mahi to Hawaiian guitars and the lilting harmonies of "Lovely Hula Hands." The scent of gardenias and frangipani wafted through the soft, blue South Pacific night.

Like a lei tossed in her surf, I had come back to Hawaii. I had heard her call early in life, even before those magical days on Waikiki during college. Now Amy, too, had fallen under her spell.

Churning through the towering surf along the cliffs of the wild Na Pali coast in a "zodiac boat" was a favorite adventure. The twenty-four-foot speed raft had no keel; it was designed for the expeditions of Jacques Cousteau to maneuver in and out of narrow, shallow coves. On our first zodiac boat trip, we were speeding toward home with our Shaklee traveling companions Bob and Juliette Stevens, running against the wind and the tide so that the seas were piling high. I was seated behind Amy, the last in the line of our foursome, as we rode the slender inflated rubber bench on the outside of the boat. We bounced high with each wave and had to hold on and "post" as best we could as we came back down, and we all laughed and whooped like cowboys. Suddenly, I was no longer there. I had raised up when I should have sat down. In a split second I was in the air, then plunging into the high seas, narrowly missing the propeller as I shot downward.

It took a while before anyone noticed that I was no longer on board. By then, the boat was zooming far ahead, and I found myself alone in the violent seas of the Na Pali coast, gasping for air as wave after wave crashed down on my head. Although a strong swimmer, I found myself tiring quickly under the beating, and instantly understood why even strong swimmers drown. With everything I had, I struck out through the heaving waters toward the disappearing boat ahead, surprised by how little progress I was making, hoping they would see me, stop, and make it back to me before I went under. By the time the boat swung around and began speeding back, I was weakening rapidly in the pounding sea. It looked like the distance they had to travel was so great that by the time they reached me it might be too late. The thought came, coldly and clearly, that I just might not make it. As I struggled to keep my head above water, the boat drew closer and closer until at last, hands reached out to grab me and hoist me aboard. I had escaped watery oblivion in paradise.

Despite such close calls, every year Amy and I, together with the Stevens, would seek out a skipper who might still be game to operate a zodiac boat. With the dubious reputation of the boats, it wasn't always easy. We pulled Captain Jack from boozy retirement out of a motel phone book.

"How in hell did you find me!? Sure, meet me down at the docks at 10 a.m."

We brought a small wad of cash, and the day's supplies of lunch and sunscreen and met our skipper and his aged, but seaworthy craft. Captain Jack, probably in his late fifties, was leathery from the tropical sun; his voice was croaky from a hangover, and he was prone to salty quips and a roving eye toward Amy and Juliette. The five of us set out with the wind at our backs on a gentle, rolling sea past the towering, sheer green cliffs of the Na Pali coast.

There were beaches hidden between those cliffs that were forbidden to the public, so naturally, we asked Captain Jack to sail into them. Happy to visit one of his secret haunts, he slowed down the motor, and lovingly coasted us into Eden. The white sand beach ahead was devoid of human footprints, and multicolored birds flitted between the slowly swaying palms. As the craft glided silently into shore over gently rolling waves, the five of us looked at each other and without a word, we took off bathing suits and slid into the warm, crystal-clear water. Startled fish swam by to inspect us, and dolphins played farther out. Emerging from the sea on that pristine beach, we knew we had fallen through time and space into a paradise on earth. Words were unnecessary, and all we could do was smile giddily at one another, seduced by the sun and the sea and the scent of the trade winds.

After our first time on Kauai, it became our custom on subsequent trips for Amy and me to start out early in the morning on the Kalalau Trail, which passed close by our lodgings near Kee Beach on the Na Pali Coast. We packed sandwiches and water and walked into the lushness of old Hawaii, where the pristine, empty beaches of the Hanakapiai Valley waited at the end of miles on the trail.

A shady canopy of coconut palms cooled us as we pushed through ferns, banana plants, philodendron, red hibiscus, pink ginger, and cream-colored passion flowers. After an hour we halted at a clear, rushing mountain stream, where a rope had been thoughtfully hung for the passing hiker. Taking turns, we grabbed hold and sailed across. From there, the trail climbed out of the jungle and up a sheer ridge. Rain-soaked gullies cut across the trail, and we grasped at exposed roots for support. When we reached the summit, we caught our breath and surveyed the scene below—the turquoise blue Pacific rolling onto a vast expanse of white sand, dotted by pools and boulders and populated by only two or three swimmers. On the descent down to the beach, we laughingly gave up looking for footholds and surrendered to the slippery slide through the mud to the valley below. There we swam in the blue ocean and lay still on white sand.

In a hidden cove on Kauai, in the depthless eyes of a wolf, in the last stand of a rat, there are moments when the veils part and we glimpse inexpressible beauty and mystery.

To see a World in a Grain of Sand
And a Heaven in a Wild Flower
Hold Infinity in the palm of your hand
And Eternity in an hour...
—William Blake, "Auguries of Innocence"

CHAPTER 13:
KINDERGARTEN FOR ADULTS

Mitakuye Oyassin – "We are all related, two-legged, four-legged, furred, finned, feathered, in the soil or growing from it."

—Lakota proverb

Suddenly, Jean Huston was speaking directly to us from the car cassette player. "Imagine you are on the road to new hope...." We literally *were* on the road to New Hope, Amy, Rory and I, in search of a new home. We'd heard of the little town on the Pennsylvania/New Jersey border called New Hope, and its colony of artists, writers, musicians, and theatre folk. While we cherished the old farmhouse on Van Auken Creek—the trees, the garden, our animal friends—the area was a cultural desert, and our spirits were fading. The synchronicity of Jean's shout out wasn't lost on us.

The recording was from one of Jean Houston's Mystery School weekends, sent to us by Amy's sister, Dody, who'd been an attendee and who had been trying for some time to interest us in attending. Like her sister, Dody had a keen mind and a wildly imaginative sense of humor. They made a formidable pair.

As it turned out, we never did find a house around New Hope, but Jean's eerily timed message finally prompted us to check out the Mystery School, and for this we would be eternally grateful to Dody.

In October of 1996 we attended the "guest weekend" in a pastoral setting near Port Jervis, Pennsylvania. We were hooked from the start. "Kindergarten for adults" perfectly describes the rich, hilarious, mystical weekends of high play called the Mystery School. One minute you might be hearing a presentation on quantum physics; the next, you're up dancing it into your body/mind to thundering rock 'n roll, or singing a Dylan song led by Gerry Dignan, Jean's music director. You might be engaged with a partner in a guided "mind game" process that Jean had devised, or be caught up in a Shakespearean scene with the actress Peggy Rubin, Jean's multi-talented assistant, or find yourself charging down the meadow in a game of Quidditch, a la Harry Potter. Then you and a hundred other attendees were off to an animated, high octane organic lunch in the adjacent room.

The fellow participants were all accomplished in their own right— teachers, writers, painters, musicians, scientists, UN workers, ex-nuns, Buddhist devotees, therapists of all stripes. Sometimes Loretta Afraid of Bear with her Mohawk husband Tom, her mother Beatrice Long Dance, and a few Lakota from the Rosebud Reservation would join us.

Dr. Jean Houston, a pioneer in the humanistic psychology movement, has authored many ground-breaking bestselling books—*The Possible Human, The Search for the Beloved, Life Force,* and *Jump Time,* among others, and a riveting autobiography, *A Mythic Life.* The Mystery School was Jean's adaptation of the ancient mystery school traditions of Egypt, China, and Greece. She incorporated traditional dances and ceremonies as well as zany, brilliant innovations of her own. It was an exuberant celebration of life, a fearless exploration into our human potential and the mysteries of the universe, and a far cry from the woods of Pennsylvania.

When Amy emerged from the first weekend immersion, she started drawing again, something she hadn't done since teenage years. The fallow fields of our psyches seemed to stir and quicken. It was as if our lives had cracked open and deepened. Mystery School reignited my singing. It inspired Amy's writing, and helped her reimagine her work at the Karen Horney Clinic. It galvanized us both to want to vacate the backwoods and move full speed ahead in fulfilling our lives.

I had done my best to keep vocally active while living so far from New York. A fifties a capella doo-wop group in Scranton called "The Nostalgics" asked me to join them. For an a capella group, blending voices with exact pitch is imperative, and the Nostalgics faced an unusual challenge. One of our four members was deaf in one ear. Needless to say, we each had to step up our game. In the end, everyone's musical skills benefitted.

We managed to turn out some fair tape recordings and did a jingle for the local radio DJ. We also opened for a couple of rock 'n roll nostalgia shows in the Scranton area with former fifties celebrities like the Duprees, the Shirelles, the Platters, and others. A highlight for me was jamming with the Platters at intermission to their enthusiastic nods and smiles.

Mystery School became the centerpiece of our lives for fifteen years, and, together with Dody and occasionally Norman, their adventurous dad, we didn't miss any of the monthly weekend sessions during that time. Every year Jean chose a different theme, such as "The Mystic Path" or "The Way of the Artist" or "The Hero's Journey." Each month, she chose a particular figure as the focus. Provocative reading suggestions helped us to prepare. The weekend might be centered around William Blake, Francis of Assisi, Ramakrishna, Shakespeare, Mozart, Leonardo da Vinci, or Jean's mentor, Margaret Mead. It might be based on Lincoln's Gettysburg Address or on the mythological themes of *Star Wars* or the Harry Potter series. For the weekend on "Bodisatvahs" (mortals who have reached a state of enlightenment and choose to remain here on earth), we brought the Lindwalls to the Mystery School.

Apart from enlightening weekends at Mystery School, we were fully engaged in our lives. Amy was drawing more and more recognition for the depth of her work at the Karen Horney Clinic. At the same time, we continued to help people live healthier lives with Shaklee's products and income opportunities. Sometimes our efforts took us into unknown territory. Through referrals, we were led to an African American family in the Brownsville section of Brooklyn, an area marked by sudden violence and gang warfare. The nutritional supplements were producing some major health results and people there had begun telling others about it. The family was eager, warm, and welcoming when they called on Amy and me to come down and help guide their burgeoning Shaklee enterprise.

After driving to Brooklyn, we were met by five muscular young men in red and black berets who escorted us silently and alertly to the apartment building in Brownsville for the meeting. Many of the people we met there were dealing with conditions such as diabetes or cardiovascular difficulties. Sometimes they had to share bottles of supplements, having only a few dollars to spend. Health meant that much to them.

Over the course of our monthly treks to Brownsville, our friendships with the people there deepened. From time to time, faces would disappear from the gatherings. One week they were among us, the next they were gone. Some died from lack of medical care. One young man was shot in the entranceway of the building. While Amy and I reeled in shock, the hardship and tragedy of Brownsville were all but taken for granted by the people living there. Although we did our best to help establish a foothold of health and security there, in the end we were unable to overcome the odds. We cherished the people we had grown close to and were deeply grateful to have seen a world most people will never know.

Dody continued to be a conduit for bringing pivotal figures into our lives. The "spiritual intuitive" and mystic Myron McClellan, along with Jean, was her most significant find. There were times when Amy and I felt called to see Myron and tap into the subtle mystical realms he was rooted in. Like Doc and Ruth, Myron would become family, and we would see him in Denver whenever we visited Dody at her home.

During the first years of our marriage Amy and I were ambivalent about having children. The most we seemed to manage was agreeing to be godparents for Julian, the newborn son of Amy's college friend Alice. While we had some connection with Julian in his early years, our lifestyle ultimately left little room for involvement.

Something within me knew that I, for one, was not meant to have offspring. I wasn't sad about it. I even joked that it took all my energy just taking care of myself—or to use Amy's memorable phrase, "the care and feeding of Richard." Amy on the other hand, while hesitant, still longed to have children, and I wanted to honor that. By the time we started trying, however, the biological clock had almost stopped ticking. To our astonishment, we discovered it was too late. We never could agree on adoption, so Amy quietly carried a sadness and longing for a child all her life.

Our connection to animals was another matter. Before and during life with Rory, there was a succession of stray cats that gravitated toward our home and found our cellar. First there was Buster, the noble, lion-like cat reduced to scratching out a life under porches in Honesdale, until he crept into Amy's arms. Then there was MacDuff, who appeared on the lawn one summer day and rubbed against Amy's leg. His fierce, defiant independence was at odds with his devotion to Amy. Later came sleek, black and white Kathumi, with the blue eyes and a penchant for roaming. There was odd, "touched" Willoughby, and small, wide-eyed Cosette, abandoned in a Kmart parking lot. Malachy, with a damaged hind foot, found his way into our dirt cellar. While upstairs talking on the phone with her sister, Amy heard a faint meow coming from somewhere below in the house and remarked nonchalantly, "I guess we have another cat."

Then there were the delicate long-nosed deer mice, looking exactly like the illustrations in Beatrix Potter's books, who popped up and stared at us from the stove burners. Knowing they would soon be cat fodder, we caught them in "Have-a-Heart" traps, and they lived like royalty for years in aquarium tanks decked out with the trappings of their natural environment. There were the baby rabbits we watched for weeks beneath the Swiss-chard leaves in the corner of the garden, and the full-grown black rabbit we rescued from the prison camp conditions of a neglectful neighbor's yard. He spent the rest of his short life on our screened front porch facing the creek. One Sunday morning as I came downstairs, I heard desperate squeaking. I swung open the door to the porch to find a weasel clinging to the rabbit's back, struggling to get to his neck through the fur. I quickly reached down and, with effort, plucked the weasel off of the rabbit's back and placed him on the floor. He scurried through an impossibly narrow opening in the screen and ran down the embankment to the creek. The rabbit was unfazed, but I'd come downstairs just in time.

Amy with rescued rabbit and Buster, the king cat.

There were the cedar waxwings who taught their young how to fly from our maple trees. The adults hopped from limb to limb, high up in the tree, letting out encouraging chirps to the baby bird frozen on the limb below. When the juvenile jumped off, he was airborne for a few seconds, then floated heavily to the ground amidst an exchange of frantic chirps from his folks higher up. We found a broken branch about twelve feet long and propped it against the tree, then watched as the baby climbed back up the trunk to safety. The watching parents cocked their heads at this, then chirped encouragingly to junior, who would try his wings again momentarily.

There were the two baby rabbits we rescued from a nest ravaged by a neighbor's dog. Amy dubbed them "Cowslip" and "Peas Blossom," in homage to *A Midsummer Night's Dream*. Only a few inches long, they fit contentedly in the empty match boxes Amy prepared. With exquisite care, she coddled them to robust health until they were large enough to return to the wild. Holding them close to her breast, she carried them, one at a time, to the edge of the meadow and gently set them down. They stood motionlessly for a moment, noses twitching, marveling at the possibilities of the vast expanse of grass and bushes before them, then bounded away into the brush. The following spring, we spotted a full-grown rabbit slowly hopping through our yard, stopping now and then to twitch his nose. We liked to think it was grown-up Cowslip or Peas Blossom, returning to the scene of a happy childhood.

For years, Rory had been the official Mystery School mascot. He loved being taken on his ceremonial walk around the closing circle at the end of each weekend. Some of the red fur around his face had turned white now, and he passed more of his days sleeping on his couch in the living room. One day on his way to the water dish, his legs gave way, and over the next two days, his water consumption increased, and his stumbling grew more pronounced. The vet said Rory had kidney failure. We prepared to take care of him for as long as it was tenable.

The phone rang. It was Jean, who evidently had cut short a meeting with some official, because she'd heard Rory was in trouble. Like us, Jean seemed to be part dog. She had even written a book, *Mystical Dogs*, about her succession of wondrous canine companions. Years earlier, when she heard that Amy's sister Dody didn't have a dog, she had exclaimed, "How can she stand it?" For Jean, dogs sometimes took precedence over high-level meetings. She not only loved Rory, but she knew how close the three of us were.

"This is what you do. Look him straight in the eye, and you tell him to come back in a strong, healthy body."

And that's what we did. We got down on the floor nose to nose with him, looked him in the eye, and choking back tears, repeated the mantra until we knew he'd gotten it.

In those last few days, we camped out with Rory. We rearranged the downstairs for his comfort, carrying him out in the autumn night, slowly coming to grips with the inevitable. He moaned almost continually now, and his suffering was unbearable for all of us. We called our vet, who had attended to Rory down through the years and was like family. She pulled into the driveway Sunday morning with her bag. Through tears, she gently administered the shots, and in the moments of Rory's passing Amy and I felt a lifting and a lightening in the room, and within.

We willingly embraced Jean's healing myth of animal reincarnation and began to check in regularly with the vet and the local dog shelters for newly arrived puppies. But in none of our puppy encounters did we feel any special connection.

At Mystery School for the next few months, we always checked in with Jean. "Downloads" from the spheres were a regular part of her life, but so far she had nothing to tell us.

"Is he in a body yet?"

"Not yet."

Then one day, "He's getting ready to be born somewhere...but I don't know where."

Months later she declared, "He's been born."

Now we focused. We checked with shelters wherever we traveled in Pennsylvania and New York. When we visited Doc and Ruth at their home in Hot Springs, Arkansas, we checked the shelter there.

Back home again in Pennsylvania, I drove down the road to our vet. I had just been there two days previously for supplies but had forgotten to pick up cat food. I walked into the clinic and, in a tired monotone, recited to the young vet tech the stock phrase I had used so many times before:

"I don't suppose you have any puppies, do you?"

Suddenly, the air shifted. "Puppies!?" she exclaimed, her eyes widening, a smile beginning. "Just a minute!" She disappeared into the back where I heard quick muffled exchanges and a burst of bright laughter, and then "Oh, perfect!"

She returned with a second techie and the same vet who had come to the house months before to help Rory move on to his next plane of existence. All three women were beaming silently, while I stood in a kind of haze. Half asleep in the doctor's arms was a puppy of astonishing beauty, not six inches long, with blazing white fur, one blue eye and one brown eye. The vet, clearly the "gatekeeper" in this story, placed the tiny white pudding in my arms without a word and stepped back, eyes sparkling. The puppy stretched lazily, met my eyes, and promptly settled in to sleep.

As I stroked the soft fur, still in a haze, I stammered, "I-I don't understand. I was here just a couple days ago, and you didn't have any puppies."

Then came the lightning bolt: "Oh, she was thrown out of a car on Route 6."

The phrase might as well have been code. "Thrown out of a car on Route 6" was the exact wording a vet had used twelve years before to describe what had happened to Rory. It was a kind of cosmic confirmation, and my head swam.

I contained my excitement and waited until evening to call Amy at the apartment after she was back from the Karen Horney Clinic. I described the details of the encounter as neutrally as I could, without trying to influence her. When I got to, "She was thrown out of a car on Route 6," she yelped, and I could see her jumping up and down in the apartment. That phrase sealed it for both of us.

We named the puppy "Leela," after the "miracle plays" at Sai Baba's ashram. As she grew, it became apparent that her temperament couldn't have been more of a contrast to Rory's. Whereas Rory had been quiet and angelic, Leela was feisty and exuberant. We wondered at first how our serene Rory could have morphed into such a radically different personality. What could possibly surpass angelic? Why, joy of course!

As we got to know Leela, we began to be able to differentiate between personality and soul. While the personalities of the two dogs were a stark contrast, we saw that the soul was the same.

Leela grew into a sleek, stunning, white-furred combination of what appeared to be golden retriever and corgi, with some basset hound mixed in. With one blue eye and one brown eye, and her startling white coat, she stopped pedestrians in their tracks when we walked her in New York. A year later, in the days following 9/11, she was an emissary of healing. Our walk around the building, which usually took fifteen minutes, took almost an hour, as person after person stopped to caress her, marvel at her beauty, and breathe out their grief to this big-hearted, four-legged angel.

In the days following the terrorist attack, we were saddened to see people of Middle Eastern ethnicity sometimes being harassed. Amy and I made our way down to the Twin Towers site to find a Middle Eastern restaurant we could patronize. The Lebanese restaurant we chose was already feeling the effects of a customer boycott. It was the dinner hour, and we had the restaurant almost to ourselves. The gratitude and humility of the owners was heartbreaking. We left as generous a tip as we could, and told friends about our experience, hoping they might also patronize Muslim businesses. It is unlikely our little restaurant survived the weeks that followed, but we knew we had at least done what we could.

Leela succeeded Rory as the official Mystery School dog, and we were frequently asked to share the wondrous story of her "reincarnation."

Leela and Kathumi, best friends.   "A peace that passeth understanding."

As the new century opened up, we grew more determined in our search for a place that would better match our expanded spirits, a place that also was mercifully closer to New York City. A house in the Hudson Valley appeared on the Internet listings that looked promising, and we drove the two hours from Pennsylvania to see it. A rambling center-hall colonial built in 1765 with wide plank floors, the house sat on land that had once been a farm. There was a bearing chestnut tree, wild raspberry and blackberry bushes, and an open, sunny meadow perfect for a large garden, bordered by a low stone wall and state forest.

Situated in the tiny hamlet of Thompson Ridge near the village of Pine Bush, the house was a full hour closer to New York City. We were so taken with it that we rushed forward to draw up the papers, before realizing that we wouldn't have the funds to buy it until we first sold our house in Pennsylvania. We realized we had to let it go. Like so much in this story, the house would appear again, at the right time.

At Mystery School a friend walked by carrying a book entitled *Extraterrestrial Contact: The Evidence and the Implications.* I hurried after her to ask if I could take a look at it. As I quickly scanned its pages, a tingling sensation rushed up my spine. I immediately ordered a copy.

When I was a boy of five or six, living in our house in the little town of Western Springs, Illinois, I had an experience that didn't make sense. The incident took place somewhere around 1946. I remember somehow being out in space amidst the stars. Suddenly the stars zoomed in toward me, then zoomed back out again. In and out, a couple of times. I don't know whether I was dreaming when it happened or awake; whether I was physically "in my body" when it happened or "out of my body." Either way, I remember that the image was vivid, that it was a mystery, and it has never left me. Since the experience "didn't compute," it would stay unacknowledged and on a back shelf of my mind until decades later.

It was near the end of our time in the house on Van Auken Creek that the memory was suddenly triggered while watching a History Channel documentary on the Roswell affair. And now, as I began to turn the pages of this matter-of-fact, entirely credible little book, I was on the verge of a wondrous, life-changing odyssey.

Mitakuye Oyassin (all our relations) was about to acquire an unexpected new meaning.

CHAPTER 14:
WITH WONDER IN OUR EYES

Let me wander through the meadows of the teeming midnight skies.
Let me feel you walk beside me there, with wonder in your eyes . . .

RICH FLANDERS, "MIDNIGHT SKIES"

It is one thing to believe we are not alone in the universe. It is quite another to experience it. In the spring of 2000, I participated in the "Ambassadors to the Universe" training with Steven Greer, MD, in the Hudson Valley of New York and was ushered into a new reality. It was as if I had stepped off solid ground and into empty space.

I knew of Dr. Greer after reading his book, *Extraterrestrial Contact: The Evidence & The Implications*. Unlike many books about UFOs, this one was compelling and credible. The evidence seemed verifiable, and the book had an explosive impact on my mind. At the end of the book is a word about the Ambassadors to the Universe trainings, which venture into the field and successfully make contact. Having long been drawn to the mysteries of the stars, I decided to invest the time and funds to gratify my curiosity and do the "training" as soon as possible.

As part of the registration process for the project, participants were required to sign a form stipulating that no hallucinatory drugs, alcohol, or stimulants of any kind were permitted during the seven days of the training. That was not a problem for me, as I wasn't drawn to stimulants or hallucinatory substances, my one adventure with LSD notwithstanding.

We were also required to sign a release form, stating that in the event we were given the opportunity to go aboard a "craft," we did so totally of our own volition, and that we released the organization of any and all responsibility. After much gentle haggling with Amy, I assured her that I would not go off into the unknown and abandon my responsibilities here. But I knew this was the most wondrous opportunity life would ever offer. I couldn't imagine turning it down. I never told her, but I signed the form.

In the afternoons, during seven days of classes, we explored the new physics, the history and nature of the UFO phenomenon, the history of the "cover up," and experimented with remote viewing. Our nights were spent out under the stars on the sprawling field of an abandoned farm, where we practiced the guided meditation process given to Dr. Greer for "vectoring in" prospective visitors.

On four of those six nights, immediately following that vectoring-in process, we saw craft of various shapes in the skies above and around us, and on one occasion, I experienced a "close encounter of the fourth kind." This is defined as "a UFO event in which witnesses experience a transformation of their sense of reality" (*Unacknowledged*, Dr. Steven M. Greer, page 233).

That encounter went something like this. We had just completed the meditation and were standing up for a brief break. Dusk was approaching, and as we gazed out into the field and forest beyond, Steven suddenly exclaimed, "Oh, look! There's a partially materialized craft!" Quickly setting aside the unfamiliar concept of "partially materialized," I looked in the direction of his pointed finger. Sure enough, about a football field away, there was an unmistakable grey, cottony, bowl-like shape sitting amongst a stand of trees. My heart leaped, and without a moment's hesitation, I commenced walking rapidly toward it, remembering to open my palms at my sides to show I was unarmed, as Steven had taught us. He was walking with me, slightly behind and to my left.

The memory of what followed next would come back to me sporadically in the days and weeks after the encounter. I don't remember much about the actual walk, only that I had stopped abruptly when I was perhaps twenty or thirty feet away from the foggy shape in front of me, and I recall that, for some reason, Steven was no longer there with me. I was only yards away from a cottony grey mass that looked like a bowl or cup, or the bottom half of something oval-shaped; it was about thirty feet high and about as wide. Inwardly I knew I could advance no further. I had come as far as I could, and now the next move, if there was to be one, would have to come from somewhere else. In silence, and alone, I stood in the presence of something entirely unknown.

Since I felt blocked from going further forward, I could only go inward. I closed my eyes and immediately felt myself become immobilized. At that instant, a being about four feet in length plastered itself diagonally across my chest. My eyes were closed, so this must have happened, at least in part, on an inner plane. Yet, I also felt the physical sensation of being fused, cell to cell, with this being. As I dimly recall, the being was hairless, with large round eyes—though not as large or opaque as those in the popular pictures of "aliens," and he seemed to be male. He telepathically asked something that took me completely by surprise, the last thing I would have expected.

"Will you protect me?"

Dumbfounded and immobilized, I couldn't reply in that instant, but I would have answered, *"Yes, I'll do what I can."*

I don't remember more. I don't recall returning to the group, and yet I seem to recollect being with them for the rest of the evening. Somehow, I didn't mention this experience to anyone—or even clearly recall it—until days and weeks afterwards. It took a while for me to realize that I had experienced a "close encounter," because the form it took was so unexpected.

The week had begun with an experience almost as extraordinary. On that vast stretch of abandoned farmland, somewhere between Newburgh and Pine Bush, New York, two dozen teachers, businesspeople, engineers, students, scientists, and people of all sorts had gathered at dusk to form a circle on the grass. Dr. Steven Greer, the project leader, introduced the nature of the work we would be doing. He explained that each of us was integral to the discoveries and knowledge of the whole, and that whatever any one of us saw, felt, smelled, or heard was to be conveyed to the whole group.

I had traveled far to participate in this training. I would be away from Amy, our home, our animals, and our Shaklee business for a week. I had spent a couple thousand dollars to be part of this, because I deeply resonated with the spirit and goals of the project: to make peaceful contact with what were possibly interstellar visitors. But on this first evening I was played out from the stress of the trip, questioning why I had done such a foolish thing. I felt about ready to go home. Inwardly, I asked for guidance, a "sign" of some sort, that I'd done the right thing. Almost immediately, I felt the inclination to turn my head, and right there in front of me, inches away, a patch of ground lit up like Christmas. Jumping exuberantly up and down in the grass were about a dozen shimmering red lights, finger length. My jaw dropped open as I gazed at the spectacle of little red dancing lights, transfixed. I managed to turn away long enough to stammer to the guy next to me, "Did you see that?" But when we turned back to look, the lights were gone.

Remembering that Dr. Greer had instructed us to share whatever we saw, I collected myself and raised my hand to relate what I had just experienced. Remarkably, no one else seemed to have seen what I had, although the people directly across from me in the circle would have had a clear line of vision. Without missing a beat, Dr. Greer replied, "Oh yeah, those are the ETs who followed me here."

Now, I prefer to think they also followed me there, because the feeling they projected was one of welcome and celebration. Old friends?

So began a week-long journey of wonder and adventure.

Later that same evening, Dr. Greer led us through the "vectoring in" meditation process for the first time. Incredibly, as soon as we opened our eyes, there they were. Two white buttons among the stars, motionless, not twinkling, seeming to be waiting for us to notice them. The moment we did, they came alive, zooming at impossible speeds and madly zigzagging across the sky—and then suddenly vanishing. It was as if they wanted to make sure we all saw them, to assure us that it wasn't an optical illusion. Then, just as suddenly, one reappeared directly overhead, descended slightly, and burst into bright bloom, a glorious white flower... then vanished. The intent was clear—a spectacular "Hello!"

There are more things in heaven and earth, Horatio,
than are dreamt of in your philosophy. – Hamlet

It was far too late to call Amy that night, but I couldn't contain myself. I woke her up, jabbering about what I had experienced. Sleepily, she indulged my rant, understanding that this first evening of the training had already been life changing for me.

Two or three nights later, one of our participants, an engineer, commented that he had somehow missed seeing anything. "You people all see these things. I never see anything!" he complained good-humoredly. Standing on a hillock, about a dozen of us, including the gentleman who had so far missed out, did the vectoring-in meditation process again. It was a quiet spring night, fragrant with blossoming meadow flowers, under a clear sky glittering with stars; the Big Dipper was almost directly above us. Suddenly from the edge of the horizon there emerged a triangular shape with a light on each point, floating silently across the middle of the sky. Speechless, our gazes locked on the soundless, majestic triangle gliding overhead. Tears sprang from my eyes and ran down my cheeks. Upon reaching the exact center of the Big Dipper, the craft stopped dead, and then slowly turned clockwise (or maybe counterclockwise) on its axis; slowly and deliberately it made one complete revolution. The message was unmistakable. It was acknowledging our presence and saying hello. Then, just as before, it slowly and soundlessly glided across the sky to the opposite horizon, where it disappeared as abruptly as it had appeared.

Our engineer had finally had his sighting. The group burst into a flurry of excitement and fell deep into wonder.

One night, immediately following the appearance of craft overhead, we heard the clatter of helicopters and the roar of jet planes. They streaked across the sky and we found ourselves under the searchlights of hovering helicopters. We weren't trespassing on government grounds; we were private citizens peacefully reaching out to welcome what apparently were off-world visitors. Yet powerful beams of light shot down persistently from the helicopters in an effort to disperse us. We didn't budge, and the helicopters finally departed. This incident opened our minds to the possible credibility of the "conspiracy theories" about government cover up of certain phenomena.

On another evening, we had just completed the nightly routine of setting up the Geiger counter, radar equipment, and recording devices, when a fountain of sparking white light suddenly streamed up about a foot into the air from the grass in front of me, then disappeared. This phenomenon occurred at least two more times during the course of the night. Later on, the microphone from the recording equipment began to emit short crackling squawks; some high, some low on the scale. But curiously, the recording device was not turned on! We formed a circle for meditation and chanted a few "oms" in unison. Suddenly, we heard a scratchy, sustained version of this "om" sound coming from the microphones (still not turned on), as if something was trying to communicate with us by imitating us. We were struck by the humor of it as much as by the wonder and mystery.

One night the Geiger counter and the radar detector suddenly went into action; immediately we felt the air pressure shift, the temperature go down, and the woods grow silent. Steven commented that perhaps a craft was settling inter-dimensionally over and around us. We seemed to be sitting in a circle together in silent inter-species communion with non-visible friends.

Our week of wondrous events drew to a close, and we all returned to our homes. My mind swam unceasingly after the event. I felt as if I was no longer walking on solid ground—that if I put my foot out, it would touch empty space. Whenever I was outside, I automatically looked up, scanning the sky.

Realizing the enormous implications of what I had encountered, I felt an urgency to share my experiences as widely as possible. I didn't hesitate to recount my stories to anyone open to listening. At Mystery

School round tables and as a speaker at various "experiencer groups" in and around the city, I shared the story of my encounters. Speaking about the experiences also helped me to integrate them.

Soon after my adventures in the field at the Ambassadors training, I began to notice that a distinct, tiny red light would sometimes appear at significant moments. I'd see the light sitting still amid the dark boughs of a tree at night or dashing across a room. An interstellar friend?

A year after the Ambassadors to the Universe experiences, I helped arrange for Dr. Greer to do a symposium in New York. At dinner following the event, I told him about my experiences with the being from the "partially materialized" craft. He listened closely; yet oddly, he did not seem to have any particular remembrance of that night, only remarking, "Oh, yeah, that's happened to me in my life, as well." What particularly struck me was his response to my description of the cup-like shape of the object: "Oh, you only saw the *bottom* half! Probably because that's where the power center is." In other words, implying that the full shape of the craft, not visible to my eyes, was oval.

Eager to extricate ourselves from the backwoods of Pennsylvania, Amy and I had placed our house on the market. Now we had a buyer, but we had no idea where we would move. No properties were available in the areas where we had searched, and the closing date was approaching. Amy went on the Internet, and within a few moments, a house came up with all our desired specifications. The description seemed eerily familiar. The reason why soon became apparent. We realized to our amazement that this was the exact same 1765 colonial in Thompson Ridge in the Hudson Valley that we'd had to let go of a year and a half before! Incredibly, it was still available—evidently waiting for us.

The purchase went smoothly, without complications. Our hearts leaped every time we ascended the crest of the road that wound around to our new home. It stood at the top of a rise amid rolling horse farms and apple orchards, near the village of Pine Bush.

Not long after we moved into our house that summer of 2001, I began to notice familiar landmarks in the area. Then with a jolt, I realized why. This was the exact same area where I'd been a year earlier with the Ambassadors to the Universe project! Somebody was up there laughing at yet another cosmic joke. It turned out that Pine Bush had been known for years as "The UFO capital of the Northeast." Visitors with telescopes lined our country roads on summer nights, hoping to see craft in the sky.

A few years later, during the week between Christmas and New Year's, I was walking our dog Leela at around midnight. We were making our way down the quiet, snowy country road in front of our house when, directly ahead, there appeared an egg-shaped object with multi-colored lights floating soundlessly toward me in the sky. My adrenaline picking up, I telepathically sent a message of welcome. The craft stopped and stood motionless in the sky for a few moments; then it slowly backed away and faded before my eyes until it completely disappeared. My welcome had evidently failed. Or perhaps they had detected danger somewhere.

I was not the only one who had seen the object that night. Several homeowners in the area reported sightings as well, and a report appeared in the local paper. Perhaps the cottony, "partially materialized" craft I had experienced that night in 2000 with Dr. Greer's group would actually have looked egg-shaped when fully visible, like this craft.

Now, whenever I step outside at night, I look up. Since those moments of wonder in the fields of Pine Bush, scanning the heavens has become second nature.

Mitakeyu oyasin, we are all related.

Afternote

Before writing my story in this book, I had never tried to set down these experiences on paper, since they tend to be ineffable, even mystical, by nature. The events continue to tumble about in my head, and I have only shared my account with those who were curious, and with fellow experiencers at a handful of public presentations. I have attempted to capture them within the written word now, because I believe events such as these hold new promise for our world.

In my experience, our visitors are peaceful, and we have nothing to fear from them. A whole new world will be open to us if enough people can evolve sufficiently to welcome them as part of the same family. What's more, the technology for interstellar travel—apparently an anti-gravity energy source—is nonpolluting and could be used to create a sustainable planet. The secrecy surrounding the critical information that unacknowledged "black operations" projects are concealing from us must come to an end.

The wonders of the universe are just a blink or two away.

In the years following the experiences of 2000, the melodies and lyrics of a song came to me. This is the only song I have ever written, and rather than being composed by me, I feel it simply came through me.

Midnight Skies

Let me wander through the meadows
Of the teeming midnight skies,
Let me feel you walk beside me there,
With wonder in your eyes.

I only know I feel a call,
A pulsing from afar,
A longing pounds within my heart
For brothers in the stars.

And who's to say what mystery
Awaits us in the blue?
Or if they seek the mystery
That shines in me and you?

One Universe, One People,
Scattered through the stars!
The promise of the Ages,
We're becoming who we are!
Feel the glowing heart pound
In every living thing
Through the Universe...
Everlasting Love
From many stars to many lands
Have they come to lend a hand?

The lights are glowing in the sky
And from the ground on which you stand.

And on and on, and hand in hand
Across the galaxies,
The harmony of all of life,
Divine diversity

One Universe, One People
Scattered through the stars!
The promise of the Ages,
We're becoming who we are

Feel the glowing heart pound
In every living thing
Through the Universe...
Everlasting Love

And as I go along my way
My eyes'll rove the skies
And you may come and you may go,
But nothing ever dies.

The lights are dancing deep within
And soaring high above
And through the sun, and through the clouds
The everlasting love!

One Universe, one People

Scattered through the stars!

The promise of the Ages,

We're becoming who we are!

Feel the glowing heart pound

In every living thing

Through the Universe

Everlasting Love...

The everlasting love

Music and Lyrics by Rich Flanders

(Copyright 2008; recorded on the album, *Yondering – Songs of the American West* www.richflandersmusic.com)

If you wish to explore this subject further, you will find an excellent list of resources at the end of this book.

CHAPTER 15:
YONDERING

Where the sun played all day on the deep black soil of the meadow behind the house, we planted a sprawling garden. There we grew green and yellow zucchini, butternut squash, beets, carrots, swiss chard, green beans, brussels sprouts, celery, green peppers, red potatoes, radishes, onions, and three types of tomatoes. In a patch by the side door, we grew chives, mint, thyme, basil, rosemary, parsley, garlic, and romaine and butter-crunch lettuce. On some evenings in the old colonial in Thompson Ridge our entire dinner was picked only moments before.

As happened wherever we lived, critters came. In the mornings wild turkeys emerged from the woods to leisurely peck their way across the property. Ramsey, the fawn rescued by our neighbor, would amble over to graze on the tulips and snuggle with Amy, as if she were deer family. It was a delicious sensation to kneel down and put an arm around him and look into those liquid brown eyes. It was interspecies connection, not unlike a close encounter.

Thompson Ridge home in the Hudson Valley.

There was the wild, tortoiseshell cat so terrified of humans he'd run like a cheetah if he caught sight of you. We fell in love with his pluck and beauty and longed to rescue him and give him a home. That took two years of trickery and persuasion. We left food for him on the porch, which he came for when we weren't around. Eventually we were able to walk on the porch without him bolting. We erected a cardboard shelter for him there, with a blanket for the winter.

After two patient years, Amy was on the porch one spring day setting up his water and food dishes, when the desperate cat made a decision. After subsisting defiantly on his own through all seasons, and in spite of his fear of humans, he suddenly walked over to Amy and brushed against her leg. It was a breathtaking moment. He had chosen trust over fear. We were never more thrilled than to have been claimed by this magnificent creature. We named him "Ravenclaw," in homage to one of the Hogwarts houses in the Harry Potter books.

"You become responsible, forever, for what you have tamed."

—*The Little Prince*

Amy and I were active with Orange County Peace & Justice Coalition, a grassroots group in nearby Middletown that opposed some of the activities of the George W. Bush administration. When Bush, Cheney, and Rumsfeld pushed for war in Iraq, Amy and I made signs and headed out for the junction near Pine Bush to join other horrified citizens in a last-minute show of resistance, a demonstration reminiscent of the 1960s. We strung ourselves out along the highway, and held up our signs to the passing motorists, many of whom honked in support. Feeling inspired, I broke into song with John Lennon's "Give Peace a Chance," and soon the line of people up and down the road joined in. Although we were not successful, we had at least tried. Subsequently, as the unlawful and unethical activities of the Bush administration piled up, Amy and I helped draft a resolution for impeachment, published as a full-page spread in the *Herald Record*. Little did we imagine that down the road there would be someone far more dangerous in the White House, a man who would pose the greatest threat to our Constitution in U.S. history.

On a quiet Sunday evening I got to musing about the remarkable people I had known in my life—in the army, in college and high school, in various shows. I wondered what might have happened to them. After dinner I set about thumbing through old phone books, but most of the names I sought were not to be found.

I wondered what had become of Anne Tarpey. Where had life taken her? I hadn't seen Anne since we'd graduated from The American Musical & Dramatic Academy in 1970, and I had all but erased from my mind that lost, ill-fated love affair from so many years ago. I doubted she would still be in the New York phone book, and I could hardly believe it when I spotted a listing for "A. Tarpey."

"Anne?"

"Richard?"

We recognized each other's voices instantly, though over forty years had passed since we last spoke to each other. We easily fell into an animated conversation, catching up on each other's lives. I breezily told her about my marriage to Amy, our home, the animals, the Shaklee business, performing. She was warm and genuinely happy for me and the rich and soul-satisfying life Amy and I were living. I was amazed to learn that Anne had never married.

As it turned out, she had chosen a deeply rewarding mid-life career path. She had earned a masters' degree in clinical social work and spent a decade as a practicing psychotherapist. She had then moved into the field of "organizational learning" and held leadership positions in "service excellence" at renowned hospitals. She loved her work and had a deep commitment to improving the healthcare experience for patients and their families while supporting the workforce caring for them. She had launched leadership development initiatives for managers and leaders. In short, she was not just the performer I had known, but someone with major accomplishments who had a fierce heart for healing.

I wondered whether she was still at all in show business. It turned out that she had kept her hand in, creating and performing in one-woman cabaret shows for the joy of it, and as time would allow. A fan of the new sciences, she had called her most recent show, *Love, Lust and Quantum Physics!* She wove theories from quantum physics through musical gems from the Great American Songbook. Now she was researching string theory, the next frontier.

The girl I had known all those years ago was not just a gifted performer but had turned out to be a leading light in health care, a healer, and a brainiac.

Vividly remembering her performances as a singer and actress, I mentioned Broadway Concerts Direct, the collection of former and current Broadway talents that musical theatre legend, Sarah Rice, had created. I was performing with the group in and around the city, and I wondered if she might be interested in connecting with Sarah.

By chance, I had called Anne on the eve of her moving out of the city. After residing in New York for almost forty years, she would be leaving the very next day, having accepted a senior healthcare consultant position at an international research and consulting company in Washington, DC. It was an amazing synchronicity. She had planned to leave no forwarding number, so if I'd called just one day later, we would not have connected.

Before we hung up, I secured her email address to add to my contact list to send her announcements of my future concerts, along with political messages and posts on animal causes. I suggested in passing that if she ever returned to New York we might all have dinner together.

In an unlikely phone connection, a beam of sunlight had been cast onto a deeply buried memory. The murky past was being exhumed and transformed into something bright and untroubled. It was a revelation hearing how Anne had become such a light in the world, and I felt happier as I went forward with life.

Mystery School had churned up our creativity to a high pitch. To honor my folks' connection to the Big Band era and the Great American Songbook, I partnered with a marvelous new singer, Celia Berk, and Alex Rybeck, one of the finest pianists and musical directors in the business, on a show called *Double Standards*, which played at Don't Tell Mama, a cabaret in New York. When we recorded three songs from the show for an album of the same name, we were delighted to discover we'd captured some moments of true musical magic.

For years I had also wanted to honor the songs of the West that had been such a huge part of my life. Now I determined to create an album that would pay tribute to that music, to Amy, and to all the wild creatures in "songs of earth, sky, and the great lone places." I set about co-arranging them with Ken, my producer, and recording them with guitar, fiddle, bass and accordion accompaniment. Because we were not likely to find a trio of backup singers trained in the music, I did my own harmonies.

While Amy and I were trying to come up with a name for the album, I told her about the two golden retrievers I'd loved in Rhode Island at Theatre by the Sea. They would romp down the beach, dashing in and out of the breakers. One of them had a name I'd never forgotten, "Yonder."

"That's it!" cried Amy. "Yondering!"

We'd found the perfect name for the album, and we may also have invented a new verb.

I'd been singing the songs ever since hearing them performed by the Sons of the Pioneers in the Roy Rogers films of my childhood. They evoked the far horizons, wide waving prairies, and clear mountain pools of the West, and the beauty, peace, and primal energy of nature. The music seemed to move people, and the album was well received by reviewers and by other Western artists. The Academy of Western Artists nominated *Yondering* for Album of the Year and the song, "Blue Prairie," for Best Song.

Of all the generous reviews we were honored to receive, I was most touched by this one from "Musical Medicine," the newsletter of the Inner Harmony Health Center:

"The music of *Yondering* reaches deep into the heart, bringing a sense of peace in an unsettling world. In the tradition of the great cowboy singers – The Sons of the Pioneers, Rex Allen and Roy Rogers – these are fresh, authentic, lushly textured renderings of the most beautiful songs of the wide open spaces."

It was at about this time that we heard about the Thirteen Grandmothers. Loretta Afraid of Bear Cook of the Lakota people, who periodically joined us at Mystery School, showed up with her mother Beatrice Long Dance, a revered tribal elder. She rose to speak of a great vision. Thirteen female elders from thirteen different tribal nations around the world had discovered that they'd all had the same dream. Each of the elders shared the vision of helping humanity survive this time of great change on the earth by teaching people to live in harmony with nature. "In harmony with nature" also happened to be the guiding principle of the company I had represented for decades, Shaklee. It was a phrase we lived by.

The Thirteen met near the town of Bethel in Upstate New York. Representing Lakota, Apache, Cheyenne, Comanche, and indigenous peoples from Peru, Thailand, the Arctic, and Africa, the Thirteen sat in an inner circle. Surrounding them in a larger circle were those from other cultures who'd been drawn to Bethel in support of the vision. Among those sitting in that outer circle was Gloria Steinem, who rose to introduce herself saying, "I'm from the tribe that's lost its memory."

The International Council of Thirteen Indigenous Grandmothers became the subject of a documentary called *To the Seventh Generation,* and they traveled around the world teaching the age-old wisdom of their people to white civilization. But influential doors were still not opening to them, and they had little funding. Jean rose to ask the attendees gathered at Mystery School, many of whom had media, publishing, and diplomatic connections, to offer what we could to this cause, if we felt moved by it. With hearts pounding, Amy and I searched ourselves for what we might be able to contribute. Neither of us was in a position of power or influence, but Amy instantly knew one thing: "There has to be a song about this!"

As soon as we got home that night, she set about writing lyrics. Ken, my musical partner on *Yondering,* heard the story and was instantly inspired. He soon came up with a haunting melody, along with more lyrics.

Meanwhile, an idea dawned on me in response to Jean's question. I remembered that we'd be flying to Dallas the following week for the awards ceremony of The Academy of Western Artists. I took my place in the line of people offering their services, and when it was my turn, I placed my hands over my heart, then extended them toward Loretta and her mother, seated on a blanket gazing up at me calmly. I smiled and said quietly:

"Mother, I love your country, and I sing about its beauty. I am about to go to Texas for the ceremony that gives out awards for albums like mine. This is what I give. If I win the award, I will use the moment to tell all those people about your work. I will tell them about the Thirteen and spread the knowledge of what you are doing on behalf of the world."

A few days later, that is exactly what happened. Amy and I held our breath in that Dallas theatre when they announced the nominees for Album of the Year. But *Yondering* didn't win. When the next category was announced, Best Song, I bounded to the stage as the MC read, "Rich Flanders, for "Blue Prairie." After a breathless "thank you," I paused, and then began to relate the vision of the Thirteen Grandmothers. Many in that gathering were descendants of the settlers and soldiers who had bitterly fought the Western tribes a century ago. Perhaps a bit ambivalent about what they were hearing, they nevertheless applauded generously.

Will Rogers Cowboy Award, Academy of Western Artists, Dallas, Texas, 2009.

"Thirteen Voices," the song that Amy and Ken created, was a moving tribute that would become cut number thirteen on a new cd, a sequel album to *Yondering*. We would call this cd, *Ride Away*, after the theme song sung by the Sons of the Pioneers in the John Ford masterpiece, *The Searchers*. The Western Music Association nominated *Ride Away* for Album of the Year in 2010, and "Thirteen Voices," for Best Original

Song. At the awards ceremony in Albuquerque all the nominated songs were performed by the artists. A stillness hung in the air as the last note rang in "Thirteen Voices." As in Dallas, the audience was made up of seasoned Westerners whose ancestors had struggled savagely with Native Americans earlier in our history. They sat in silence a moment longer, then burst into enthusiastic, extended applause. Piercing the old barriers of race and resentment, "Thirteen Voices" evoked the land that all of us, white and Indian, loved and shared, and a moment of grace and healing descended on the audience. It was as fulfilling an artistic experience as I've ever had.

Thirteen Voices

Thirteen voice speak out loud and rise above all others
Send a message strong and proud and call the Earth our Mother

In the land of Iroquois, Thirteen found a plenary
Western sisters joined them from, the tribe that's lost its memory

Children heed your Mother's cry, her heart is surely breaking
Time so quickly passes by, there's too much left worth saving

Chorus:
Save thee, oh! Indigenous ones, precious daughters and your sons
For seven generations long, your children must be strong
When you're not here for them....survival will depend
On what they take from you....and who they pass it to

Lawyers for our Mother Earth come from the four directions
Hand in hand this song to birth...We are all relations

Sweet Mother Nature's on the run, but life is worth sustaining
Give us wisdom, everyone, to act in the time remaining

Chorus:
When our children's children find some day, a world where they belong
Ever grateful they must stay to thirteen voices strong
Ever grateful they must stay to thirteen voices....proud and strong

Music by Ken DeAngelis; Lyrics by Amy Ober and Ken DeAngelis (Copyright 2009, recorded on the album, *Ride Away*, www.richflandersmusic.com)

Months later we received a request from the Thirteen Grandmothers, who were holding their international gathering that year in Washington state. They asked if we could please send them thirteen inscribed copies of the song with a brief dedication. I was as stunned and honored as if we'd been recognized by kings or queens of Europe. For to me this was true royalty.

"To the Grandmothers....
From the heart of our Mother Earth, this song is dedicated to you on behalf of all our relations – two-legged, four-legged, finned, feathered, furred,
and all the rest – in deepest gratitude. Mitakuye Oyasin.
Rich, Amy, Ken"

CHAPTER 16:
IN THE DARK

Now in his late eighties, Doc's health was failing in 2008. He and Ruth were residing year-round at their lakeside home near Hot Springs, Arkansas. While on the phone with him, we asked if he had any special thoughts to impart. "Get neutral," he breathed. Those were the last words he ever said to us. Doc passed shortly after that, but his words would remain etched in our minds. His luminous spirit is never far away.

Over the years, Amy's presence at the Karen Horney Clinic had gradually transformed it from a cold, cerebral, paternalistic environment into one that was more heart centered. By 2012, she was highly regarded in the field for her work with the most challenging patient cases. In addition to her psychotherapy practice, she was now the head of the Trauma Treatment Center at the Clinic, so she stayed at our New York apartment on Tuesday and Wednesday nights. We would drive in together from our country home on Tuesday morning for her to start her three-day work week. I'd drop her off and return on Thursday in time for a voice coaching session before meeting her for dinner. Then we'd drive back to the country for a four-day week together.

On a sunny, cool, Tuesday morning in November we were completing our usual preparations for the drive to the city. It was almost time for us to leave and I couldn't find Amy. I walked from room to room calling her name, and then I went outside and called again. Still no answer. I began to realize that something was amiss. With a chill, it dawned on me that while searching through the house I had only glanced quickly in our bedroom. With pounding heart, I ran back up the stairs and walked further into the room, where I saw her lying between the wall and the bed. Bellowing her name, I ran to her and grasped her limp form in my arms. Shaking her and continuing to call her name, I rang 911. They told me to pump her chest until the EMTs arrived. But she was gone. A hidden coronary condition had run its course.

We had shared the same heart, and in those times when the world had seemed too much to bear, we were one. Now I was half.

In black grief, unmoored, I groped my way through the stormy winter months that followed, vacantly going through day-to-day tasks. There seemed no end to the weeping that wracked my body, and in some moments my mind slipped toward oblivion.

Then one day a therapist acquaintance looked me in the eye, held my gaze, and spoke slowly and deliberately. "You've had a traumatic shock." She paused, still holding my gaze, and added quietly, "You're still in shock."

Having it stated so starkly helped me begin to integrate what had happened.

For a few weeks Amy's sister Dody and I were able to channel our emotions into preparations for what would be an enduring memorial for Amy. It was presided over by Hal Robinson, a close friend who was also a treasured performer in the American theatre. Friends and relatives gathered from far and near, along with Amy's fellow therapists from the

Institute. Their stories and anecdotes of being touched by Amy brought her vividly to life. Amy's simple, physical presence had awakened something in people. That the world was to go on without her, without that healing presence, seemed inconceivable. Our performer friends expressed their feelings in exquisite, carefully chosen songs. Jean Houston had prepared a moving video tribute, and by the time the ceremony concluded, the collective grief had begun to flow into a glowing, indelible remembrance.

My sister Sue and Amy had been close. Within days of Amy's passing, Sue had dropped everything and flown from her home in Idaho to quietly, efficiently, and selflessly assist me. In addition to Sue and the friends and neighbors who called and stopped by, there were those less visible, glowing from other realms. The wolves, the rat, and the endless critters we had lived among were there, too. And always there was the great elm. "All our relations."

And then there were the "grief groups."

The social worker assigned by the coroner's office recommended a list of these groups that met at various locations nearby. Perhaps I could attend a group meeting and see if it might be helpful.

The group I selected was held in the office of a clinical social worker in Middletown. It was midweek, around the dinner hour, and only the social worker and a secretary were still in the building when I walked in. He was kindly, soft-spoken, and respectful as he asked me to tell him what had happened and how was I doing. As we sat there and I began to talk, I couldn't help but notice as the clock ticked on that he and I were the only ones in the room. He casually said that he was expecting a couple of others, but we should go ahead. After I got through my story, a bit shaken at living it again, it was still just he and I in the room.

"Well, let's wait a bit more."

Having said my piece, we sat in silence for about five more minutes. Finally, it was clear that no one else would be joining us, and we stood up to leave.

"Next week, same time. Should be people joining us then."

Next week, same time, I spruced myself up and drove down to the office, looking forward to finding some degree of illumination or comfort from the group. Once again, he and the secretary greeted me in the office. He was as resolute as the first time, all set to begin, as he beckoned me proudly into the room where the group was to meet—which once again was empty. He and I were going to be "the group." I was not about to repeat the experience. I thanked them both and said I was sorry but that I would have to leave. Quietly and somberly, they bid me goodbye. So ended the Group of One.

The next group meeting on the list was held at a church in a village about twenty minutes away. This group met in the evenings, and it was open to all. I arrived a few minutes after the session had begun and was ushered into a room with perhaps a dozen women seated at a long table. There was a vacant chair at one end. I put on a smile of greeting and tried to make eye contact with everyone at the table, but without success. As I took the seat, one of the ladies walked over and placed a pencil and open "workbook" on the table in front of me.

"We're on page 67. See? Right there," she said, returning to her chair.

The woman across from me was gazing down and speaking very softly, something about losing someone.

"Well, what does Paul say about this in Ephesians 1?" asked a steely, middle-aged woman at the end of the table in a flat tone. "Let's look at the bottom of the page."

Assuming all present were in abject grief, I continued to try to make eye contact, but no one acknowledged my presence, let alone met my eyes. Every face at the table seemed tightly shut. No feelings of pain, anger, or grief were about to pop out. The ladies frequently turned to the leader at the end of the table to provide guidance via the "workbook."

An hour passed, and I might as well not have been present. No one had said "welcome," no one had asked me what had happened, no one had met my eyes. As everyone donned coats and got up to go, I remained as invisible as when I'd entered the room an hour before.

Strike two.

Not willing to give up, I circled another group on the list, one that purported to be "spiritual" in nature. They too met in a church, but at 7:30 in the morning. That meant getting up pretty early, but I was game.

I drove up to the church in the gray January cold, the tires crackling the sheets of ice in the parking lot. I saw no signs, so headed for the nearest door. Farther down the lot another car pulled in. A gray-haired lady in a beat-up overcoat emerged and shouted, "Lookin' for the group?"

I followed her down the steps into the church basement, and we walked along a dim corridor past musty offices and a dank kitchen. I heard chattering further down the hall, and we walked into a pantry-sized room with a card table and five older people standing or seated around it, bundled up in the unheated room, drinking coffee from paper cups. An open box of powdered donuts lay amidst the crumbs and grease stains in the center of the table.

"Hi," I said, trying to be hearty. "Is this the grief group?"

A long-haired fellow in his seventies looked up, startled to see a new face. For a moment he was speechless, then he beckoned me: "Yes, yes! Come on in."

"Hi. My name's Rich." After they went around and introduced themselves, I expected I'd subsequently be asked to say something about what had brought me there. I managed to get out that my wife had just died, suddenly and unexpectedly. Then the old fellow next to me grabbed my shoulder, looked intently into my eyes, and said that he'd been with the group for seven years, and that nothing had seemed to change. He said I'd "get used to it." I smiled politely, and before I could speak further, the leader began to hold forth, pointing to the coffee-stained papers spread out on the table.

"Now, Rich, this is the way it works. This is a chart showing the steps. Right now," he said, reaching across the table to point with his pencil, "this is where you're at."

I couldn't make out the fine print, but some things were already becoming clear. "And this," he said, his pencil landing decisively on another page, "is where we're going to get you."

I was asked no further questions. Apparently, I had been accepted as a new "member," and the five of them continued to exchange banter, complaints, and old stories while I sat there, smiling politely every now and then. We never took off our jackets, the coffee grew cold, the donuts vanished—and apparently, nothing changed. You accepted your fate and didn't expect anything better.

Strike three.

"Grief Groups" would make a good tale.

On a biting cold January night, as I opened the front door to take Leela out for her final walk before bed, I remember absently noting that the coyotes were yelping more frantically than usual. As we trudged down the empty road, snow crunching underfoot, the coyotes and all the night creatures suddenly went silent. Turning around to walk back to the house, I looked up and saw an enormous half-moon, bright yellow orange, hanging over the road. I hadn't noticed a moon in the sky earlier. Steadily gazing at it as Leela and I walked back up the road, I slowly began to realize there was something different about this moon. Not only was it an odd orange color, it seemed to sparkle faintly. The instant that I realized that this was no moon at all, the shape began to slowly fade, dissolve, and finally disappear.

From somewhere among the stars, friends had come to call.

Once again, the night was still and moonless. Dazed, I entered the house, realizing I had just been given a great, kind blessing, a beautiful reminder of something far greater than my dark night.

CHAPTER 17:
FLAME OF DESTINY

"To tell you the truth, what feels best right now is sitting on the couch with my old dog, with the snow coming down, reading *The Girl with the Dragon Tattoo*."

"Yeah, that and a ham and cheese on rye for you and your doggie."

I laughed out loud. It was only a few months since Amy had died, and I was still ragged. But something sang inside as I read Anne's one sentence reply to my email. I smiled to myself, "She gets it."

The memorial for Amy had taken place two months before, but Anne had only just seen my email announcement and had kindly sent her condolences. I hadn't seen her in forty-three years, but after our brief connection by phone some years earlier, I'd put Anne on my email list serve for events and announcements.

In the darkness following Amy's death, friends and family tried to help, recommending books and grief groups. But these had done little to bolster me. For all intents and purposes, life was done. I passed through each day mechanically, caring for Leela and our cats, slowly going through Amy's belongings, tending to the Shaklee business, and keeping up the voice as best I could for the monthly concert performances with Broadway Concerts Direct. Singing was something I could do. The concerts gave me a purpose and sparked a glimmer of hope in my life. But I couldn't help but notice how my spirits lightened when exchanging emails with Anne.

Anne was now living in White Plains, New York, having left Washington, DC, to resume hospital-based leadership work in a multi-hospital regional trauma center.

I wrote her an email suggesting that we finally have that dinner together. In my devastated state there was no thought of "romance." I was a raw soul following a ray of light up from the darkness. I only knew that the thought of having dinner with Anne somehow brought a spring to my step, and for me, that was water in the desert.

It was February 16, 2013—two days after Valentine's Day, Amy's birthday, and a little over ninety days since she had died. Anne and I hadn't seen each other since graduating AMDA in 1970, and I wondered what she would look like now. The memory I had from so long ago was of a dark-haired, Irish beauty with laughing eyes.

I had chosen to meet Anne for dinner at Sarabeth's on 83rd and Amsterdam on a Saturday night. That was where Amy and I had always celebrated her Valentine's Day birthday, our anniversary, and other special occasions. It never failed that, upon arriving at Sarabeth's, the only table available for Amy and me would be a certain booth in the rear, the coziest spot in the restaurant. We came to think of it as our special place. Someone up there was smiling, because this evening would be no different. When I walked in, the restaurant was packed, but the waitress exclaimed, "I have just the spot!" She ushered me to that very same booth, and there I waited for Anne.

"Richard?" I looked up into a pair of merry eyes, and a face as beautiful as I'd remembered it. I felt I was being lifted as I rose to my feet and our eyes met. From that moment on, nothing would be the same. It was as if forty-three years had never happened.

I barely remember what we ordered. From the moment we sat down, we seemed locked in on each other, and we didn't get up from the table until the restaurant was in the process of closing, four breathless hours later.

Leaning forward, our eyes sparkling, we were astonished to discover that our lives had followed parallel paths, nearly crossing, for over four decades. It was a tale so unlikely that a publisher of fantasy novels would have rejected it.

We learned that the first time our paths almost crossed was back in 1970, soon after we'd left AMDA to go our separate ways. I did a summer stock production of *110 in the Shade* at a theatre in Brownsville, Pennsylvania. One month later, Anne came to that same theatre to do *Wait Until Dark*. Strangely, we'd never noticed each other's names on the posters. At the Barn Dinner Theatre in Jackson, Mississippi, it was the same story. We were totally unaware that after I had performed in the show *I Do, I Do* there, she came in with *The Fantastiks*.

Our mouths dropped open when we discovered that Anne had frequently visited someone at the West Side Manhattan building where

Amy and I had our apartment! Every week for four years she had come to see an ill friend who lived there. And yet in all that time, we'd never once crossed paths in the lobby or in the elevator.

Next, we learned that when Amy and I were living outside the tiny town of Honesdale, Pennsylvania, home of the Himalayan Institute, Anne, who was a member of the Institute, had regularly attended weekend classes and meditations. Not once during the fifteen years Amy and I lived there did Anne and I run into each other on the main street of town or on the grounds of the Institute.

One of the most amazing "coincidences" of all was that while Anne was studying for her master's degree in Clinical Social Work at NYU, Amy was there at the very same time studying for the same degree. They may have sat in the same classrooms, yet they never knew one another. Both of them became psychotherapists specializing in the same field, trauma.

Anne subsequently went on to a rich and varied career developing innovative programs in patient care for several top hospitals, and currently held a leadership position at one of them.

If ever there was a tale of serendipity, and how we're not fully in command of the paths we're on, this was it. Clearly, the unfolding story of Anne and me was one of wonder, mystery, and whimsy. I began seeing the play of our lives as a graceful cosmic comedy.

I looked into the depth of her eyes and said, "We'll have to do this again."

Outside on the sidewalk, a wide-eyed kid, I hugged her, laughing. "You're wonderful! I love you!"

"I love you, too!" she exclaimed merrily in reply.

In that moment we were two guileless children. And with that I waved goodbye as she settled into a cab. As she later described the ride home, "For the first time in my life I felt completely serene. Something came to rest, like somehow I had come home."

As for me, the walk down Columbus Avenue to the apartment was more like floating. I felt light yet grounded at the same time. All the long drive home to Thompson Ridge my head spun with the dawning of new hope. I was swimming up from the darkness of three black months. Although I awoke the next morning in the same desolate bed, I now had the fresh memory of a bubbling happiness. I could never go back. Joy was possible, and I could not, would not, ever forget it. Anne, and memories of how I'd once felt about her, came tumbling upward.

We agreed to have a second dinner, this time at Anne's place in White Plains.

"But I'm bringing my dog!"

"Okay. I love dogs."

Somewhere along the way I made a wrong turn, and I pulled over to call Anne on my cell phone.

"I'm sorry, I might be a few minutes late. I got lost."

A slight pause, then a calm voice. "Richard, it's alright. We have the rest of our lives."

Startled by her own words, she would wonder where they had come from at the start of second date!

For a moment I was stunned, then a warmth spread through me as I quietly replied, "That's right, we do."

I knew. We both knew.

Upon entering the apartment, Leela stopped a moment to look at Anne, circled the room once, then decisively laid down on the rug in the middle of the floor. The new lady had passed the test.

Leela, my old companion, seemed right at home, and I was feeling that way too. Seeing how comfortable Leela was and not wanting to disturb her, Anne suggested that instead of going out, she could make dinner there. Nothing seemed more natural. She happened to have the ingredients for a wonderful vegetarian pasta dinner. Within a few moments of being together in the apartment, all three of us were at home.

As the winter sun descended, we sat side by side at the table in the candlelight, with a spectacular view of the distant city from her 23rd floor windows. Leela slumbered contentedly, as we continued to unfold the story of our lives since AMDA. We moved to the couch, and soon I found myself telling her about *Shane* and the meaning this story had held in my life. I even ventured to tell her about my ET experiences. She was still, her whole being listening.

She talked animatedly about her work and her passion for healing, alluding to innovations in health care delivery she had created that clearly were of significance. Her varied talents and accomplishments were an ongoing revelation. But the magic of the night was unfolding in the silences and bright glances into each other's eyes.

Then Anne said, "Remember the letter you wrote me after my father died, that you handed to me at the funeral?"

It took a moment, but then I recalled how I'd thrown myself into composing that letter, working on it almost nonstop for a day and a night. It was designed to express everything in my heart that I knew I would no longer get a chance to tell her.

"I saved your letter all these years. I wanted to find it the other day, and as I started to search, the very first box I reached into – I couldn't believe it. There it was, right on top! Richard, it is unbelievable. The angels are having a ball."

She handed me the fading, perfectly preserved envelope from forty-five years ago. The handwriting was so careful, so clear and legible, that I barely recognized it as my own.

"May I open it and read it? I hardly recall what I said."

It took several minutes to silently read the message from so long ago, a message that was finally being answered in this softly lit apartment glowing with rekindled love, forty-five years later.

On our third date, I brought my cds, *Double Standards, Yondering,* and *Ride Away,* to share with Anne, three creations that held deep meaning for me. As we played the music, Anne didn't just listen, she seemed to live inside each song.

Later, I interrupted an animated conversation and blurted out, "We are getting married, aren't we? Aren't we?"

We looked deeply into each other's eyes, suspended in the knowing of the moment.

"Yes, we are."

"But not right away."

"No, not right away."

Without missing a beat, our conversation continued.

I already knew, after three rich weeks together, that we were perfectly matched—that "all our chakras were in alignment," as I confided to a friend. We didn't need a lengthy period of time to validate that. My feelings were solid and deep, yet as merry and light as any high school kid in love for the first time.

By nature, both Anne and I were independent, used to being in charge. One afternoon we took a nap together. We awoke sometime later to find our noses touching. Speechless at first, we quickly burst into laughter. So much for aloofness. As a friend later quipped, "You're two peas in a pod."

Ruth, who had lost Doc just a few years previously, paused a moment after I told her about Anne, and then observed, "Richard, most people have only one Beloved in their lifetimes, if they're lucky." In a voice that was almost prayerful she said softly, "You've had two."

CHAPTER 18:
APACHE VOWS

The day came in spring when it was time to bring Anne to the house in Thompson Ridge. I'd realized soon after Amy's death that I could no longer live there, dear as it was to me. For months I had been cleaning out the house in preparation for a move, because it was clear that Anne and I would need to find a home of our own. But it was important to share with her this beautiful place that had been so much a part of my life for the past twelve years.

Anne was exquisitely sensitive to the sacredness of the home I had shared with Amy, the years of love and joy, as well as the grief it held from her loss. Now Anne and I had to undergo our own inner journeys. Mine involved navigating through grief and time. For Anne it meant learning how to be in the space that had been Amy's and my home.

We awoke that morning to a bright May sun. Anne offered prayers of gratitude for finding each other again and asked for blessings on our journey together that day. We were ready.

The magic began as we slowly pulled into the gravel driveway. There under the towering, ancient lilac stood a young deer, not much older than Ramsey had been when Amy used to sit with him in that very same spot. A very special welcome seemed to have been arranged.

As we walked through the front door, three cats—quirky, scrappy Malachy, petite Cosette, and the fierce, magnificent survivor, Ravenclaw—slowly emerged from around the corner of the kitchen to silently survey the newcomer. Ravenclaw, who had literally only known Amy and me, and who would run like the wind from anyone else, peeked around the corner and froze when he saw Anne. This had been a wild, traumatized animal who, after two years, had finally dared to trust us and enter the house. As time passed, he and Amy had become inseparable.

Anne was instantly smitten with all of them but knew to allow them the time they needed. She was also gauging the success of the bi-weekly cat allergy shots she had been valiantly receiving over the past several months. As a Leo, she had always loved cats but had suffered from allergic reactions in the past. Fortunately for all of us, the shots were holding.

A natural with animals, she sank down on the kitchen floor, holding Ravenclaw's gaze and not saying a word. The cat's curiosity finally vanquished his caution, and he did something he'd never done before. With his eyes wide and locked on Anne, he slowly stalked toward her. He stopped dead still in front of her, looking intently at her face, then ventured one paw out to her knee, letting it rest there while continuing to stare up at her. For a time-stopping moment they both remained motionless. Then Ravenclaw made another of his pivotal life decisions. He began to slowly climb up her chest, until his face was less than an inch from hers, his wide eyes never closing.

"Richard, what's he doing?!"

"He's reading your face."

And from that moment on, Anne was Ravenclaw's beloved.

A while later he beckoned her up the stairs to the room Amy and I had given him when he'd first come into our house in order to quarantine him from the other cats. He approached the room, then walked back to Anne. He repeated this a couple of times.

"What's he doing?"

"He's showing you his room."

"He has his own room?"

"Yes."

Ravenclaw escorted her in, first showing her his food and water bowls. He then leaped up to his bed where he happily got some quality cuddling from his new best girl.

I began to show Anne the house. As she would later describe it, the house seemed filled with a golden welcoming light, the Keeper Spirit of the home, leading us from room to room, an unfolding presence of pure love. The cats followed at a distance.

In early June, when I strode into the village jeweler in Pine Bush to see about a ring, I had yet to formally propose to Anne. I planned to do that sometime later in the summer, maybe on her birthday in August, and I carefully composed the words I would say. Meanwhile, carrying the ring was burning a hole in my pocket, and there were months remaining! I began to envision some sort of family gathering to commemorate the event, and I would frequently ask Anne, "Are your brother and sister-in-law around? I thought maybe we could have dinner together." But they always were out of town, or otherwise unavailable. The ring, meanwhile, was growing hotter in my pocket every day.

Much to our shared joy, Anne started singing again and was now a beloved performer in our Broadway Concerts Direct ensemble. For our upcoming concert on the last Saturday of June, I toyed with proposing to her at dinner afterwards. Our friends would be there as witnesses. After all, they were "family." But as the evening progressed, no moment seemed quite right.

Cast of Broadway Concerts Direct, Fall 2013
Bottom row (left to right): Celia Berk, Carole Demas, Sarah Rice, Anne Tarpey. Top row, L to R: Mark Planner, Janice Myerson, Matthew Martin Ward, Rich Flanders. Not present: Janice Hall, Alexandra Frederick, David Vernon, Rob Gardner, Joanna Morton Gary, Eric Sedgwick, Edd Clark, Sue Matsuki

We drove home to Anne's apartment in White Plains, where I was now living part of each week. It was about one in the morning when we arrived. Looking back on that night, a kind of slow-motion trance seemed to descend on us the moment we walked through the front door. Anne later said she found herself doing something she had never done before. Standing at the kitchen counter in a kind of daze, she slowly removed her jewelry, while I absently fingered the box in my shirt pocket and began to move toward her. I found myself in front of her, a blank look on my face. We gazed at each other silently as I reached into my pocket for the box. Still mute and staring, I held the hinged blue box in front of her, my prepared speech for the occasion hopelessly gone. She looked down as I eased open the box, revealing the classic, round, diamond engagement ring nestled within. I stammered superfluously, "It's a ring."

In the lingering silence that followed, I gazed at her dumbly. She blushed and then she whispered, "You're supposed to say something. You're supposed to say some words."

My mind snapped back, and I recalled a few of the words I'd created for the occasion.

"Will you do me the honor of marrying me?"

She beamed yes! We hugged, kissed, and laughed, and to her astonishment when I slipped the ring on her finger, it fit perfectly.

During these months, I was once again learning that a human being is far more than we suppose. To my astonishment, I found myself experiencing the joy of love and the devastation of grief at the same time. That I could hold both of these all-encompassing states simultaneously was amazing to me.

The depth of grief and the impact of "traumatic shock" had stripped me for a time of the thin veneer of social appropriateness. I was as unguarded and open as a child in my interactions with people. It was as if the dross had drained away, leaving a naked self, a little like Gandalf in *The Lord of the Rings* walking into the fire and coming out the other side cleansed and translucent. In time, the vestiges of social appropriateness crept back in, but much of it had been shaken loose, and I had stretched into a greater freedom. I began to notice that my humor had grown more imaginative, and that I slipped easily into wildly inventive "improvs." I had groped my way through impenetrable blackness and come out the other side.

As if moving out of Thompson Ridge, cleaning out the Manhattan apartment, and preparing for a wedding weren't consuming enough, we had also decided to put together a cabaret show that would take place during the middle of the wedding. We asked our performer friends to choose songs that best expressed how they felt about the miracle of love, lost and found. Penny Penzner, a gifted actress who had not only been our AMDA classmate but one of our closest friends during that time, would be the perfect choice to bring our story full circle and provide the "toast."

My sister Sue and Anne had taken to each other immediately and were fast becoming true "sisters." At the special dinner on the eve of the wedding, her eyes sparkling just like when we were kids, Sue recounted to the guests a memory I'd all but forgotten. Back in 1968 I had sent her a letter about a special girl I'd met. In my letter, I told Sue that I'd found "the one." As she noted, I had never written her about a girl before.

With sister Sue.

In early December over two hundred of our friends and family members converged on Abigail Kirsch's Tappan Hill, the former Mark Twain mansion overlooking the wide Hudson River in Tarrytown, New York, for a wedding designed to open hearts and unleash joy. Anne and I wove our favorite traditions as well as our families into the ceremony. No one other than my sister could be my "Best Person." The Tarpey family had come full circle from 1968. My new brother-in-law Robb and I had in fact become like brothers. He would give Anne away, while her sister-in-law Patty acted as matron of honor. Anne's grandnieces were flower girls, and her nephews and nieces as well as my godson, Julian, all had their roles. A priest, a minister, and our companion in spirituality, Hal Robinson, all shared in presiding.

As if orchestrated, a family of deer suddenly appeared through the windows, gazing at the gathering from the snow, while singers Sarah Rice and Celia Berk began the ceremony with the haunting "Flower Duet." Anne and I then invoked the Cherokee Wedding Pledge:

Great Spirit, we honor all you created as we pledge
our hearts and lives together.

We honor Mother Earth and ask for our marriage
To be abundant and grow stronger through the seasons.

We honor fire and ask that our union be warm and glowing
With love in our hearts.

We honor wind and ask that we sail through life
Safe and calm as in our Father's arms.

We honor water to clean and soothe our bond
that it may never thirst for love.

With all the forces of the universe you created,
We pray for harmony as we grow forever young together.

First Corinthians followed:

"....And now abideth faith, hope, love, these three;
But the greatest of these is love."

A soaring "Ave Maria" was sung by soprano Julie Ziavras, followed by a reading of the prayer of St. Francis:

Lord, make me an instrument of your peace,
Where there is hatred, let me sow love,
Where there is injury, pardon,
Where there is doubt, faith,
Where there is despair, hope,
Where there is darkness, light,
Where there is sadness, joy...

As the ceremony reached its climax, no one, not even the other participants, knew that Anne and I were going to sing our wedding vows to each other. Tears and sudden gasps accompanied our trembling delivery of "Love Me Tender." Before we stepped off the dais to walk down the aisle together, everyone rose to intone the Apache Wedding Blessing:

Now you will feel no rain,
For each of you will be shelter for each other.

Now you will feel no cold,
For each of you will be warmth for the other.

Now there will be no loneliness,

For each of you will be companion to the other.

Now you are two bodies,
But there is only one life before.

May beauty surround you both on the journey ahead
And through all the years.
May happiness be your companion always.

Go now to your dwelling place
To enter into the days of your life together,

And may your days be good and long
Upon the earth.

In the cabaret at the wedding.

CHAPTER 19:
LOST AND FOUND

One day in January, after we'd returned from a snowy, snug honeymoon on Cape Cod, Leela struggled to her feet. She had been gradually failing for months, and now she could hardly stand up. I got down on the floor in front of her, and then she did something that she'd never done before. She looked at me steadily for a long moment, and in those clear eyes was not just goodbye, but kindness, sadness, and a timeless knowing. She was letting me know that it was ok. She remained standing with her eyes looking into mine a moment longer, as if to emphasize the communication. Then she sank back down on the rug again to rest. A few days later, she was gone.

She and Anne had bonded deeply in the eleven months they'd been in each other's lives, and Leela had stuck around long enough to see that Anne and I were okay. She departed in peace, held by Anne and me, swept along on waves of love on her journey. She seems always nearby.

At the beach, sandy nosed.

We had searched for months throughout the lower Hudson Valley and north of the city for a home, and although we'd seen many fine places, none of them struck us in the solar plexus. Anne was inspired to call Leigh Ann Loggins, a psychic friend who had been uncannily accurate and reliable over the years.

Without even knowing why we were calling, Leigh Ann's first words to us over the phone were, "Your guides are saying you need to be by the sea!"

Light flooded our faces. Anne and I both had fond memories of the New England shoreline from our summer stock years; Anne at a playhouse in Maine, and I at Theatre by the Sea in Rhode Island. We loved the bracing New England climate and the whole coastal region. For us, heaven was swimming in the ocean. But we knew we could never afford to live by the sea. That was for wealthy people. So we hadn't bothered looking on the shoreline.

The call ended, and Anne hustled to the computer to look at the New England coastline. We wanted the distance from New York to be no more than an hour and a half's drive. Instantly, a small sliver of the Connecticut shoreline appeared with a string of tiny towns: Branford, Guilford, Madison, Clinton, Westbrook, Old Saybrook, Old Lyme... We began scrolling through the listings, and to our astonishment, many were within our price range.

The first realtor we dialed turned out to be a perfect fit, and after only three weeks of driving up to Madison, we found our home. Toward the close of a Sunday afternoon, we were growing tired, but within moments of walking into the grey-blue Cape, our hearts were pounding.

"How far is it to the beach?" we asked the agent.

"Which one? There are six, and they're all about five minutes away."

We could hardly believe it.

Later, when we looked at the calendar, we saw it was February 16th—a year to the day of the anniversary of our dinner at Sarabeth's. The cosmic comedy continued.

The house was only an hour south of Theatre by the Sea. The dream of living by the sea that we'd both cherished for so many years was coming true.

We now were part of a small New England town, with the characteristic First Congregational historic white church commanding the village green; a picturesque main street lined with an independent bookstore, an arts cinema, a library, an Audubon store; and charming shops and cafes.

One end of town led to a long stretch of white sand and rolling breakers that was the town beach; the other side led to vast Hammonasset Beach State Park, with three more beaches, hundreds of species of birds, and over four hundred acres of marsh wildlife. On summer mornings when we plunged like seals into the crisp sea, we could hardly believe where Spirit had placed us.

We saw how deeply people were moved by our story whenever we shared it. Anne set about writing and producing a series of seasonal story concerts that wove our love story through song selections from the Great American Songbook. With the gifted Matthew Martin Ward as our musical director, we called the show *Lost and Found,* and it was soon booked at various private clubs and vibrant senior living communities on the Connecticut shoreline and in the Hudson Valley. The tears, smiles, and glowing hearts of our audiences affirmed our efforts. "You've given me hope," people would tell us afterwards.

With Matthew Martin Ward,
Valentine's Day show.

"A Touch of Jazz" Concert
with Donn Trenner.

Serendipity graced us, once again, when we met the great jazz piano legend, Donn Trenner, who happened to live nearby. Donn had been a member of the Les Brown Orchestra and had served as musical director for Steve Allen, Bob Hope, Lena Horne, Eartha Kitt, Shirley MacLaine, Nancy Wilson, and Ann Margret, among others. Studying and performing with him was like working with the Master of Music. A deep affection between the three of us blossomed, and we soon became like family. Eventually, he would become our musical director. Blending our voices in a Gershwin duet with Donn on the keys, breathing with us and weaving colors through the song, we were "in the zone." In the audience, hearts were opening, and we were at one with our purpose.

Donn Trenner

ANNE AND RICHARD FLANDERS

**A COZY FIRE
SOME TINSEL AND YOU!**
Swing and Jazz
Concert

DONN TRENNER
Musical Director

Sunday, Dec 15 at 2 pm
Concert, Cocktails, Buffet: $34.

MADISON WINTER CLUB
251 Boston Post Road
Madison, CT

Reservations: (203) 245-7934

With Donn, Madison Winter Club.

Pleasant Valley and *Malabar Farm,* Louis Bromfield's elegiac accounts of reclaiming his family farm in Ohio, had sustained me through the dark days of "alphabet city." They had transported me back to a bucolic boyhood in Illinois. Now, Anne surprised me with a spectacularly thoughtful birthday gift—a trip for two to Malabar Farm, now an Ohio State Park. Those idyllic meadows, hills, and ponds had only been a glowing picture in my heart. Now we were actually going to step into the reality.

We rounded the bend of the narrow dirt road, just as in the book's opening, and beheld a picture-book setting. Nestled in the rolling terraced hills of "Pleasant Valley," the sprawling house and white barns rose out of the landscape. Walking on this land, Anne and I fell under its spell, merging with the soil beneath. The days and nights we passed at Malabar Farm seemed somewhere out of time and space.

At last, we were under the Great Elm together.

CHAPTER 20:
TODAY

We didn't expect to be called back into action, but fifty years after the 1960s, Anne and I found ourselves doing all we could to defend the American republic against a strutting, wannabe Mussolini and his minions.

All the while we continued to sing our story of love "lost and found," bringing people hope and inspiration.

The pandemic closed off much of the outer world, but we relished the quiet as we opened and deepened to the inner world. We lingered in the chorus of frogs and cicadas at evening, the beauty of the ambling woodchuck, the antics of the catbird. The tranquility inspired Anne to create concerts online and prompted me to write this memoir.

A chipmunk stands on his hind legs, regarding me in the lounge chair.

Do I want to climb up there and eat those seeds? he inquires with cocked head, then jumps up to the cushion. The feel of his tiny feet on my palm is exquisite, as he scarfs down sunflower seeds, every now and then glancing up at me.

Though our life begins anew each day, and appears to end with "death," we seem to be more than our bodies. We seem to be part of a continuum, a great mysterious circle. And even if our most valiant collective efforts fail to sustain life on this planet in the face of climate change, and our species ends up like so many others that have gone before us, my sense is that we go on. We may think we are our bodies, our names, our careers, our relationships, but we are more. We are something indefinable, something beyond all this. Sometimes we glimpse it with the eyes of the soul.

Before us the morning sun spills across the Sound. Descending the dune, we dive into the shimmering water, Anne and I shrieking in the cold breakers as we stretch out and slice through the sea . . .

I love the earth, and each day ask Spirit to preserve and protect all life forms. I give thanks for Anne, for destiny, for this life of adventure, luck, and wonder.

But I am also a wayfarer on an open road. When the moment comes, before I go anywhere, I may wander with the wolves in the tall grass, drift with the wind in the trees, linger on the Na Pali coast, sing with the Sons of the Pioneers, keep a watch on the stars.

Then I'll put out my thumb and see what happens.

From wonder into wonder, existence opens.
--Lao Tzu, *The Way of the Tao*

ACKNOWLEDGMENTS

My eternal gratitude to Anne for her input and insights about the remarkable adventure we share. Profound thanks to my editor, Kendra Langeteig, who understood the mystical journey of inner knowing. To those who read early drafts: my sister Sue Edwards, and my friends Ed and Jill Lamoureux, Elisa Hendrey, Robertson Work, Marika Kuzma, Brenda Casey, Victoria Churchville, and Roger and Primi Carey—I'm lucky to be under the Great Elm with you.

RECOMMENDED RESOURCES

Transforming our world has never been more urgent. Here are some of the richest and most rewarding resources for exploring questions about advanced technologies, advanced consciousness, UFOs, and ETs.

The 2020 documentary, *Close Encounters of the Fifth Kind*, with Dr. Steven Greer, is critical viewing, offering the most compelling and comprehensive coverage of the subject to date. Widely regarded as the most knowledgeable researcher in the field, Dr. Greer also wrote *Unacknowledged – An Expose of the World's Greatest Secret* (2017), a riveting introduction to all aspects of the ET/UFO phenomenon, the cover-up, anti-gravity energy, and the geopolitical ramifications. Check out his other books as well, and explore the website: www.siriusdisclosure.com.

Read the equally eye-opening *UFOs & The National Security State* by Richard M. Dolan; *The Day After Roswell* by Col. Philip J. Corso, USAF, Ret.; *Passport to the Cosmos* by John Mack, MD; and *Encounter in the Rendlesham Forest* by Nick Pope. These are some of the most prominent, credible, and page-turning books on the subject.